Rural
MARKET
UNLEASHED

POSITION YOURSELF IN THE
RURAL MARKET EFFECTIVELY

SARABJIT
SINGH PURI

INDIA • SINGAPORE • MALAYSIA

Notion Press

No.8, 3rd Cross Street,
CIT Colony, Mylapore,
Chennai, Tamil Nadu – 600004

First Published by Notion Press 2020
Copyright © Sarabjit Singh Puri 2020
All Rights Reserved.

ISBN 978-1-64919-569-2

Dedicated to Farmers of India

&

My Family, Fateh Team, Our Vendors

&

Our Clients

Who Guided Me For All These Years At Every Step

Contents

Outcome

Foreword

"Rural Advertising is more of an education than advertising.
Its main objective is to improve people's lifestyle with
new ideas and technologies."

The surge in aspirations, income and the resources, in multiple ways, clearly indicates the rise of Rural India. Marketers need to understand and focus on this part of India in a different way. India's colossal rural market is an attractive preposition, but needs adequate carefulness while planning and implementing marketing campaigns. This book discusses the importance of India's rural market, its size, factors and opportunities. It also highlights government policies and initiatives impacting lives of the rural populace.

The second part of the book focuses on rural marketing strategies for products and services. With emphasis on brand building, this part touches on studying prospect behaviour and cultural diversity of rural India. Important aspects such as pricing, communication and effectiveness of advertising campaign are also discussed. The book uncovers adaptation of new technologies, women empowerment and the rise of private schools in rural India. The part also focuses on High Net-worth Individuals (HNIs) of rural India, unconventional methods of advertising, rural call centres and importantly, the advent of Digital Marketing. The author's view on maximising Return on Investment (ROI) with 360-degree sales and marketing, is explained in detail.

The third part talks about the challenges, do's and don'ts for rural marketing campaigns and specific techniques for campaign effectiveness. Taking a futuristic view, this part also comprises the role of artificial intelligence and future of rural marketing. This futuristic perspective makes for interesting read and is the key takeaway of this part.

This book is useful to many sectors, including agrochemicals, FMCG, infrastructure, apparels, electrical and electronic devices, automobiles and many more. It is a useful resource for current and aspiring rural marketing professionals.

The book summarises my views and insights from 20+ years of rural marketing experience. Hope this work is of interest and value to readers.

– Sarabjit S Puri

Acknowledgement

This work could not have been completed without the help, guidance and support of many of my close near and dear ones. I thank the farmers of India whom I have met during my travels across India. These farmers have given me the energy, knowledge and guidance regarding the agriculture and local cultures of the region. I have learnt a lot from them about the problems they are facing and the solutions they are getting. The farmers of India have always welcomed me with their open arms and hearts irrespective of the region I have visited.

I thank my parents, my mother and my father, Smt Pritam Kaur and Sh Harnek Singh Puri who have been my unconditional rock solid support at all times. Without their support and blessings this would have never have been possible. I thank my Chacha ji and Chachi ji, Mr. Sukhdev and Mrs. Gurmail Kaur who are farmers of great experience and have supported me in many ways. I thank my mother-in-law Mrs. Tara Kale for her love and blessings for my enterprising spirit. I thank my wife Pushpa for showering me with love and motivating me to follow my passion. I thank my brother and his wife Jagmeet and Navdeep for the timely support and moral strength from time to time. I thank my sisters Mrs. Varsha Kale, Mrs. Deepa Khutal, Mrs. Jahnavi, Mrs. Pratidnya and brothers Mr. Shailesh Kale, Mr. Ankush, Mr. Manish and Mr. Rajesh Mishra for their support. I thank my children Aseem, Jaskirat, Simar, Ayudh, Shirin, Sakshi, Varun, Vishwa, Sarva and Suhrudh for the pride in their eyes which have motivated me at all times to do something for them to be proud of. I am thankful to my extended family.

I am very thankful to my team Fateh, especially Mr. Vivek Singh for his kind support for more than 15 years. He has been a friend, brother and a comrade in every situation. I thank Mr. Kulwinder Khan, his association with me has been since 2005. Khan has been an excellent associate and we have done many projects together. A very honest and hardworking fellow, Tejinder Singh is also a very old associate. He has been a passionate person who has done wonders in the course of time. Thank you Iqbal for believing in my vision all these years. I also thank Ganesh, Grishma, Madhav, Mahinder, Suraj and other Fateh team members for their continuous support. All the team members of Fateh have helped me to learn many things which I have been able to reproduce in this book.

I am thankful to our clients who have been giving us a lot of opportunities in rural marketing as an agency. This experience has given me a lot of inputs for the book on rural marketing. I personally thank Mr. Ajit Chahal, Mr. Falgun, Mr. Mrugen, from Bayer, Mr. Dushyant Sood, Mr. M P Singh, Mr. Ajay Kulshreshta, Mr. Manoj Bhandari, Mr. Raghvendra Shukla from PI Industries, Mr. Neeraj Tewari & Mr. Sandeep Garg from Agrimas, Mr. Shib Shankar Ghosh, Mr. Anil P S, Ms. Rekha Nair & Ms. Heena Sharma from Isagro Asia, Mr. Ratnesh Pathak & Mr. Prasenjit Sinha from Dhanuka Agritech, Mr. Mukesh Kamboj, Mr. R K Garg, Mr. Krishan Kumar Choudhary from Coromandel Agrico, Mr. Anand, Mr. Satyajeet Singh, Dr. S S Kajal & Mr. Yogesh Sharma from JU Agri, Mr. Gulab Moorjani & Mr. Shirish Sinha from L&T, Mr. Kanwardeep Dua & Mr. Amandeep S Matharu from BKT Tyre, Mr. Rakesh Bisht & Mr. Vivek Rastogi from Willowood, Mr. J S Dhillon & Ms. Tapsaya Goel from HPM, Mr. Satish Tiwari & Mr. R K Makani from Coromandel International, Dr. Anup Kalara from Ayurvet, Mr. Devendra Kukreja, Mr. M S Bagga, Mr. H N Airi & Mr. Prashant Agrekar from Excel Crop Care, Mr. Indranil Das, Mr. Joydeb Tilak & Ms. Namita Dutt from Agrinos India, Mr. Aggarwal and Mr. Sudhanshu Srivastava from Indo Gulf Crop Science, Mr. Nikhil Aggarwal from Ichiban, Mr. Rajesh Agarwal, Mr. Inderjit Bisnoi, Dr. GP Pandey, Mr. Shishir Chandra from Insecticides India, Mr. Y K Sharma & Mr. S P Singh from Indogulf Fertilisers (Grasim), Mr. Sanjay Choudhary & Mr. Bhupinder Duggal from Sinochem India, Mr. D R Bhayana, Mr. Yogendra Arya, Mr. Madhukar Chug & Mr. Dharmesh Gupta from Bharat Insecticides Ltd, Mr. Arvind Jain, Mr. S K Sharma, Mr. Jayant Nag, Ms. Reshma Shetty, Mr. R K Bishnoi, Mr. Prakash Bhoir & Mr. Mahesh Khambeta from Indofil Industries, Mr. L R Bhayna from Sulphur Mills, Mr. Huzefa Khorakiwala, Mr. Gokul Dafale & Mr. Kuldeep Jangaid from Biostadt, Mr. Pravin Parmar & Mr. Sonal Chouhan from BASF, Mr. Ravish Jain & Mr. Ashish Panday from Savannah Seeds,

Mr. Ajeet Chahal, Mr. Umesh Tyagi, Mr. K G Krishnamurthy, Mr. Sanjeev Patyal, Mr. Falgun Shah & Mr. Manoj Varma from Bayer, Mr. Pankaj Chugh, Mr. Khantil Dixit & Mr. Deepak Upveja from Syngenta India, Mr. Satish Nartam & Mr. Pushkal Upadhyay from Deepak Fertilisers, Mr. P K Sharma, Mr. Raghu Lal, Mr. Nishin Saxena, Mr. Pradeep Kumar Sharma, Mr. Gaurav Sharma, Mr. Ankur Raj & Mr. Asad Ahmad from UPL, Mr. Prasad Pusudkar & Mr. Sangrash Khade from Swal, Mr. Deepak Singh, Mr. H P S Bhangu, Mr. S S Chandel & Mr. Raman Gupta from Gharda, Mr. Sougata Niyogi & Mr. Anil Gupta from Godrej, Mr. Anuj Sharma & Mr. Prashant Zinge from Yara Fertilisers, Mr. Pramod Kumar, Mr. Anand Dani, Dr. Surendra Roparia & Mr. Ganesh Kumar from Mosaic India, Mr. Vivek Sharma, Mr. Ravi Kunwar & Mr. Shishir Saxena from Advanta India, Mr. R K Rojara, Mr. Aseem Sharma, Mr. Kamlesh Sharma, Mr. Amit Wadhwa & Mr. Venkatesh Kulkarni from Bioseed, Mr. Vinayak Raman Sharma & Mr. O P Gupta from US Agri, Mr. Rajeev Nair from Limagrain, Mr. Tarak Dhurjati & Mr. A S Dalal from Nuziveedu, Mr. Bhagwan Das, Mr. Dinesh Reddy & Mr. Ramesh Reddy from Adama India, Mr. Jitendra Sandra & Mr. M V Rao from Nagarjuna Agrichem, Mr. Nishant Pahuja & Mr. Dharmendra Panwar from Rallis India, Mr. Devendra Singh & Mr. Praveen Panati from Atul, Mr. Arvinder Singh & Mr. Amit Dubey from Mahindra and Mahindra, Mr. Ankur Agarwal, Mr. R S Bisht & Mr. Anil Nirwal from Crystal, Mr. Kaushal Jaiswal from Rivulus, Mr. Amit Verma & Mr. Anand Gadre from FMC, Mr. Niranjan Kumar & Mr. Balakrishna M from Rasi Seeds, Mr. Shivraj Devkar & Mr. Shankar Nalwade & Mr. Atul Kadam from Mahyco, Mr. R P Sharma & Mr. Jogesh Kakar from Chambal Fertilisers, Mr. Abhigyan Rai & Mr. Gurpreet Bhatal from Pioneer Seeds, Mr. Pradeep Tiwari, Mr. Ashok Kumar Gupta, Mr. Kumar Rahul from VNR Seeds, Mr. Satinder Singh from HDFC, Mr. Gaurav Phull & Mr. Sumandeep Singh from Ceat, Mr. Girish Pandey, Mr. Chandan Panday & Mr. Milind Geete from Dhaanaya Seeds, Mr. Hari Singh Chohan, Mr. B K Singh, Mr. Himanshu Chohan & Mr. Vishwas Singh from Kaveri Seeds, Mr. Rajesh Agarwal, Mr. Surinder Matoo, Mr. Ashok Suneha, Mr. Suresh Reddy & Mr. A K Biswas from Krishirasayan. I thank all of you from the industry with whom I have worked and learnt so much.

I thank my business coaches Mr. Mahadevan and Mr. Neeraj Singh Rathore who motivated me and guided me in completing this work. The editing has been done by Ms. Sohini Ghosh with the utmost precision, thank you for that. I thank almighty for the strength and patience he has given me to complete this book. Hope you will find it useful for your future endeavours. To read more blogs by me please logon to www.SarabSays.com.

– Sarabjit Singh Puri

WHY RURAL

CHAPTER 1

Why Go Rural

"India lives in her villages"

– Mahatma Gandhi

Rural India consists of 70% of the total population as per the standard definition. But as a Rural Market Professional, it would be better described as 95% of the total market. Out of this 95%, around 25% is urban and the rest is rural. Catering to this big rural population is an opportunity as well as a challenge. The growth in rural India is fuelled by agriculture. The rise in use of fertilisers and other agrochemicals is a clear indicator of the growth in agriculture. There is a requirement of the infrastructural development to tackle the increasing yield of the crops. Road infrastructure, grain markets and other infrastructural development have been done to support the agrarian growth. The surge in industry have also helped the rural population to fulfil their dreams. With this development in the infrastructure and storage, the price and selling management have worked in a big way.

The development of private education in villages and nearby towns with CBSE and even ICSE schools have led to the development in educational standards in rural areas. A lot of awareness channels like mass media, TV channels and newspapers in regional languages have played an important role in transferring information to masses. In the last decade or so, the rise in use of mobiles and even smart phones have connected every village with the global information hubs. The role of social media, of course, needs to be discussed here in order to understand the rural market completely.

A Big Rural Population:

70% of the total population still lives in villages and around 20% in the tier III and IV cities of India. In a way, almost 90% of India is rural. Despite 71% of the country being predominantly rural, the proportion of doctors and nurses in rural areas are 34% and 33% respectively, as informed by the government to the Parliament. While over 38% of all bank branches are concentrated in urban areas, nearly 34% are in the rural areas, with the remaining in the semi urban areas.

According to a survey report on health insurance coverage in Rural India, only 14% of the rural population is insured whereas 19% of the urban population is insured. This shows a large scope for health and life insurance industry in Rural India. In a Gaon Connection Survey, every third person living in rural India (36%) prefers going to a private doctor. This clearly indicates a rise in the paying capacity of Rural India.

Agricultural Growth:

Agrochemical industries in India present immense growth opportunities. India is the 4th largest producer of agrochemicals globally and ranks 4th in terms of production of crop protection chemicals. The market in India is expected to reach US$ 7.5 billion (INR 532 billion) by FY19 and register exports of about 50% of the value of Indian crop protection industry (Source – India Brand Equity Foundation IBEF, February, 2018). Revenue growth of Indian Agrochemical companies was expected to increase by 12% to 14% between 2017–2019 (Source – Religare Institutional Research Report, January, 2017). In 2017, the market size for Indian seeds was approx. 3.6 billion dollars (INR 256 billion). Indian fertiliser market was INR 4675 billion in 2017. This data clearly indicates the growth in industry as well as in production in agriculture in India. This is certainly going to change the purchasing behaviour of rural India.

Advertising and promotional spends allocated by agri input companies towards rural promotion is approx. 2.5% to 3% of its revenue. Potential revenue of the rural advertising and promotion sector is estimated to be approx. INR 23.6 billion in 2020 (seeds and agrochemical industry).

Amongst the reasons cited for the current size of the rural market are high growth in technology and infrastructural development of the country, improvement in agri technologies and growth in yield of every crop and better market infrastructural development and godown and storage development.

One more reason is the development of big companies for procurement like Adani in apple procurement in Kashmir and Himachal and many private corporates in procurement of basmati rice in Punjab and Haryana.

Industrial and Service Sector in Rural India:

Nearly 100 years ago Dr. B.R. Ambedkar wrote, "In short, strange as it may seem, industrialisation of India is the soundest remedy for the agricultural problems of India." The rural economy is growing not just because of farming. In a paper written for the NITI Aayog by Ramesh Chand, S. K. Srivastava and Jaspal Singh, there is indication of the structural transformation of the rural economy. More than half of the industrial production comes from rural India. Rural construction also accounts for nearly half of the total building activity in the country. The value of rural services is about a quarter of the total services output.

This development of the industry and service sector across the country has led to the development of the middle classes in rural areas. Rural middle classes are now fuelling the economy of India.

Infrastructural Development:

Road network and rural electrification have not only improved the living standards but have also improved the employment opportunities in rural India. Around 97%, or 579,012 of Indian villages were electrified by March 31, 2015. A village is declared electrified if 10% of the households can access power, along with public institutions such as schools, the panchayat office, health centres, dispensaries and community centres. But by 2019, 100% villages were electrified as promised by Prime Minister Modi in 2014. However, more than 3 crore households are still in darkness, which I believe will be connected in the next couple of years. Rural roads form 73% of the 1.7 million km of Indian roads. The Pradhan Mantri Gram Sadak Yojana, a rural road networking scheme, has done wonderfully well for the connectivity of villages with the cities. But still 30% of villages with a 250 plus population are yet to benefit from the Pradhan Mantri Gram Sadak Yojana (PMGSY) in India. To boost connectivity of villages with hospitals, schools and markets, the Government of India has launched Phase-3 of its rural road programme to widen and revamp 1.25 lakh km of roads in the country. The duration of this phase will be of five years, expected to be completed by 2024–25. All these schemes will certainly make rural markets much more lucrative.

Mandis or Agricultural Markets and Market Towns in India are the hubs of economic activity. These are the places where farmers sell their produce and buy almost everything for their needs. According to available estimates, there are over 7500 regulated agricultural markets in India today, operating under different state level acts covering a huge variety of notified agricultural produce. All these numbers are the opportunities present in rural India which I have tried to present. Hope marketers will get a good insight.

Rising Standard of Education:

With this development in the infrastructure and storage, the price and selling management have worked in a big way leading to the development of private education in villages and nearby towns with CBSE and even ICSE boards leading to development in educational standards in rural areas. As per the ninth Annual Status of Education Report (ASER) released, 29% of enrolments in the 6 to14 age group are in private schools. This is a 10% increase in seven years from 18.7% in 2006 to 29% in 2013. Other States and Union Territories with a high percentage of elementary school children in private institutions include Puducherry (54.3%), Haryana (51.4%), Uttar Pradesh (49%), Punjab (46.7%), Jammu & Kashmir (45.5%) and Meghalaya (45.3%). As with private schooling, there is also a growing prevalence of private tuitions among elementary school students. The figure stands at 24.1%.

This development of schools and professional colleges in rural India have led to development of professional workforce in rural areas and the companies were able to recruit these people for work in their own home towns. This educational development has also improved the environment for entrepreneurship which have led to development of the industrial areas in smaller towns and development of dairy business and agri allied business.

Many students who have studied well have started moving outside the country to foreign lands for a better livelihood leading to more exposure to technology and developed products.

Rising Mass Media:

There was AIR and Doordarshan, then came the cable channels in the 90's which started the revolution of mass media penetration. The television actually changed the pattern of thinking of rural population in a big way. TV led to the adaptation of new technologies across the country. New ideas started flowing. According to the viewership monitoring agency, TV penetration rose from 99 million to 109 million in rural India and from 20 million to 21 million in the mega cities like Delhi, Mumbai, Kolkata and Bengaluru during this period. The survey also shows a 6.9% increase in male TV viewers (from 401 million to 429 million) versus a 7.5% jump in female TV viewers (from 378 million to 407 million).

The rise of vernacular press also came up as a revolution in print. The vernacular papers started a lot of local editions covering local news making people of rural India interested in them. The rise in local papers and papers covering specific topics like agriculture, machinery, dairy etc. also made good penetration into the market. These papers also helped companies to reach the real customers. The share of daily newspaper readers in rural areas across the country was approximately 31% in 2017, a significant rise from around 22% in the year 2014. According to the New Delhi-based Indian Newspaper Society, India has 62,000 newspapers, with a staggering 90% of them in local languages. Indian news publishers are doing relatively well, precisely "because they've spread their wings to smaller towns," says Divya Radhakrishnan, president of TME, the media division of Mumbai based advertising agency Rediffusion Y&R. But now the change of the medium from paper to internet have actually hit hard, the news through newspaper's internet sites with latest live coverages have changed the whole scenario. The use of local languages on the internet have actually worked very well for online media. Still, the newspaper penetration is increasing.

Mobile Telephony and Internet Explosion:

According to TRAI (Telecom Regulatory Authority of India) data, tele-density in rural India is growing at a much faster rate than in urban India. Mobiles, especially after the introduction of 4G connectivity, and smart phones have become popular among people above the age of 40 as well. A lot of people above the age of 60 are also using WhatsApp and Facebook. This change in the mind-set of people with user friendly smartphones have actually moved the advantage of marketing towards rural India.

Online sales have increased many folds in rural India. Flipkart said that it recorded almost 100% increase in sales to customers in Tier-III cities. During sales season, more than 40% of sellers were from Tier-II cities and beyond. Kalyan Krishnamurthy, Flipkart's chief executive officer said in a statement, "Bharat has moved closer to India in more ways than one." While Amazon India's chief says, "This has been our biggest celebration ever, a digital Bharat festival."

The impact of local language usage on the internet has changed the complete dynamics of rural marketing. According to a report by KPMG and Google published in 2017, "Indian Languages – Defining India's Internet," there were 234 million vernacular internet users and 175 million English users in 2016. By 2021, users of Indian vernaculars are expected to reach 536 million, while English users will increase to only 199 million. 90% of new internet users between 2016 and 2021 will use local languages, said the report.

The change in technology definitely gives rural marketers many things to ponder upon.

Role of Social Media:

Facebook, WhatsApp, Instagram and other media have also started their operations in local languages. Rural traffic, on these apps and sites, has increased many folds. Rural internet users have reached 120 million logging in through inexpensive devices. Using low-tariff data plans, they are sharing images and downloading songs and videos like never before. The numbers are going to surge. By 2020, rural consumers will constitute about 50% of India's internet users to reach 315 million by logging in through inexpensive devices, according to a report by the Boston Consulting Group (BCG), the US based management and business consultancy.

The surge in aspirations, incomes and resources in multiple ways are clear indication of the rise of rural India. Marketers need to understand and focus on this part of India in a different way. The colossal rural market of India is an attractive preposition but need quite carefulness while planning and implementing the campaigns. In the next chapters, we will discuss about it in detail.

CHAPTER 2

Rural Marketing – Ins and Outs

*"Rural Advertising is more of an education than advertising.
Its main objective is to improve people's lifestyle
with new ideas and technologies."*

Rural areas are opening up to new technologies and new products. With the rise in businesses, multiple channels of financing have opened up. Besides banks, many NBFCs (Non-Banking Financial Company) have also started functioning in rural areas. There are multiple types of loans that have started like home loans, car loans, tractor loans, etc. Many automobiles companies and even tractors have started their own financing divisions or companies to boost the sales of their products. Rural India is also working on its health part as a lot of multi-speciality hospitals have come up in rural areas besides normal clinics. With the rise in many sectors besides agriculture, a lot of employment opportunities have started picking up. Women education and empowerment have played a major role in building the rural economy of India. The rise of NGO's and self-help groups have also improved the living standards of many rural families.

Adaptation of New Technologies in Agriculture:

Starting with tractors to thrashers to harvesters, agriculture is becoming intensely mechanised. Farmers are now opening up to new machines which are meant for specific purposes. A lot of farm equipment and machinery companies have developed their business in the last two decades. Technologies like laser levelling of the land, precision agriculture, tissue culture and satellite based agricultural consultancy have started changing the scenario. Some of the emerging technologies that can literally change the agricultural landscape in the coming years are Soil and Water Sensors, Weather Tracking, Satellite Imaging, Pervasive Automation, Mini Chromosomal Technology, RFID Technology and Vertical Farming. Even today the electrical switches by L&T contain mobile based controls. Now a farmer can control the equipment from his home itself. Similarly in future, tractors will start indicating all sorts of troubles beforehand. Even the bacterial or viral activity in air can be sensed and whole village can use the preventive sprays to avoid disasters. The farmers are now welcoming new technologies and there is a large scope of these technologies in India. There are multiple types of equipment used in agriculture like harvesters combine, tippers, trailers, tankers, rotavators, seed drillers, oil tankers, truck containers, harvester combine, rotavators with roto seeder, hydro cutting presses, trailers, tillers, agricultural tillers, track combine harvesters, etc. These companies are growing much faster in the east and central parts of India.

Financial Institutional Support in Rural India:

Finance has always been the back bone of every business. The opening and expansion of banking services in rural India have certainly changed the game. The rate of interest has come down drastically. Secondly, number of government schemes like Kissan Credit Card have worked very well in favour of rural India. The entrepreneurs from Rural India have also got a great push due to easy finance and refinance opportunities. Online banking and number of payment transfer apps like Paytm and Google Pay is also helping the growth in rural economy. The finance of automobiles, tractors and home loans have boosted the economic growth to a large extent. Direct online payment in the farmers account is also possible because of the vast banking network expansion in rural India. There are a total 47,443 rural bank branches in around 6 lakh villages. Although a lot still needs to be done but with regular expansion of banking in rural areas, the growth will be much higher in the coming days. Even when the country is hit hard by the

Covid-19 pandemic, the rural areas are still working and could fuel the growth engines of India. Other than banks, NBFC's have disbursed a good amount of loans in these areas.

Role of Insurance:

The Indian law states that insurance companies should be accommodative of persons in the rural sector or social sector, persons in the economically vulnerable or backward classes of the society, workers in the unorganised or informal sector etc. (as specified by the IRDA). The insurance sector has also expanded its portfolio in rural India with the help of the banking sector. The budget has made provisions for paying huge subsidies in the premiums of Pradhan Mantri Fasal Bima Yojana (PMFBY) and the number of beneficiaries will increase to 50% in the next two years from the present level of 20%. As part of the PMFBY, Rs. 9000 crore (US$ 1.35 billion) has been allocated for crop insurance in 2017–18. There are many types of insurance available in rural India like Cattle Insurance, Sheep and Goat Insurance, Poultry Insurance and Aqua Culture Insurance. There are a number of private insurance players who are working in these areas with the help of the banking sector. There is a spike in health and life insurance after the Covid-19 pandemic has hit the country.

Health and Medical Facilities in Rural India:

In a Gaon Connection Survey, every third person living in rural India (36%) prefers going to a private doctor. Let us look at the figures to find out what is in store for rural India in the health sector.

In India, there is one government allopathic doctor for every 10,000 people, one government hospital for every 2,000 people and one state run hospital for every 100,000 people. The WHO report, published in 2016, said 31.4% of those calling themselves allopathic doctors were educated only up to Class 12 and 57.3% doctors did not have a medical qualification. The percentage of live births where the mother got medical attention at delivery either at a government or private hospital rose from 73.1% in 2012 to 81.9% in 2017 at the all India level. Similarly, 47% got attention before their death in 2017, up from 34.6% in 2012.

As per a survey, there are only around eight diagnostic labs per 100,000 people in India and diagnostic facilities have a very low reach in small towns and villages.

The figures are dismal but clearly shows the scope for the health care companies, hospitals and the medical testing labs. I see a great potential in all 6 lakh villages where 70% of India resides.

Employment Opportunities In Rural India:

As I have mentioned, many sectors have started growing in rural India which automatically provide huge opportunity for employment and entrepreneurship. The growth of banking, insurance, education, health, manufacturing and agricultural innovation have created huge opportunities for growth and prosperity of rural people. Advertising in rural India consisting of printing, film making, artists and implementation agencies also generate a lot of jobs. The usage of the advanced agricultural and infrastructural implements like JCB's and harvesters need a lot of skilled work force. The automobile companies like Mahindra, Suzuki and others sales and maintenance network is also generating a lot of employment. These opportunities are making rural India prosperous day by day. This prosperity is converting rural India into a big market leading to a virtuous circle of prosperity.

Rise in Women as Decision Makers:

With the rise in middle classes in rural India, the role of education has improved a lot. Now people are considering a girl's education equally important. girls have started studying at masters level and even professional levels. This phenomenon has led to the rise of women as decision makers. Traditionally, rural India has been considered to lag behind in responding to new ideas as compared to its urban counterpart. With the rise in education and jobs in nearby towns in rural India the girls and boys have started doing jobs and they are becoming independent financially. While taking the core decisions which were being taken by elders earlier like purchase of Agro inputs, seeds and fertilisers even tractors and cars, youngsters are taken into account because of their education and knowledge. Once I was travelling towards Mumbai from Punjab by train. I met a farmer from Punjab travelling to Gujrat to purchase some land. He was accompanied by his daughter. She was in the tenth class. I asked him why he was taking his daughter with him. He said "She is educated, it will be easier for me to communicate with them if she is with me"

That change of mind-set is visible and has to be taken into account.

Role of Cooperatives and Self Help Groups:

The role of cooperatives cannot be ruled out in the growth of rural economy. Cooperative movements like Amul is the one of the biggest examples. In fact, dairy and sugar co-operatives have made India a 'Major Nation' in the world with regard to 'milk' and 'sugar' production. Today, India can claim to have the largest network of co-operatives in the world numbering more than half a million, with a membership of more than 200 million. The cooperative credit facilities and distribution of fertilisers and agrochemicals have been a huge success. The cooperative sugar mills in Western Maharashtra have changed the fortunes of the farmers in that belt. Although cooperatives have failed in many parts of the country due to political interference and corruption, still this movement has changed the entire country's mind-set towards agricultural growth.

Self-help groups have mostly worked for women empowerment. In the stimulus package announced by the union finance minister to fight COVID 19, collateral free loans have doubled for women self-help groups (SHGs) from Rs. 10 lakh to Rs. 20 lakh. This will help 63 lakh SHGs covering 7 crore families. There are 44.61 lac women SHGs as of March, 2019. The following news appeared in the Tribune News Service, Chandigarh on March 6. After leaving her government job as a Mathematics teacher in the early 90s, Ludhiana based Gurdev Kaur Deol decided to empower rural women and girls. It started as a small group in the form of a self-help group and today she is transforming the lives of 300 families by marketing their produce through Farmer Producer Organisations (FPOs).

She is not a lone example. There are many women and NGOs who are engaged in transforming the lives of rural women through self-help groups. The women who were unemployed earlier are now earning anywhere between Rs. 5,000 and Rs. 20,000 per month. This income is making women more decisive and independent. Self Help Groups are building nation.

Rural marketing is the approach to see these opportunities and help people of rural India to realise their dreams and aspirations. There is a huge plethora of areas and geographies where the marketers can start, move and grow with the growing economy of rural India. Rural India is calling, "Come with us let's grow together."

CHAPTER 3

Importance of Rural Marketing

Rural India is one of the most important and biggest markets of the world. But there are numerous challenges which need to be overcome in order to understand Rural India. There is huge diversity in agriculture, multiple crops and seasonal variations. The average per capita income of India in 2018–19 was Rs. 142,719. But the variation is huge. Goa has the maximum per capita income of Rs. 502,425 which is almost 11 times higher than that of Bihar which has the lowest per capita income of Rs. 43,822 only. This shows a completely uneven development in different regions of India. This gives an immense opportunity for development of underdeveloped areas and growth in economy. The understanding of these different regions and developing different strategies would be a major challenge. With the rise in electronic media and internet usage, there is huge awareness in the masses leading to rise in aspirations. There is a sharp rise in demand for many products and services leading to job creation and the rise of the middle classes in rural India. The development of educational standards and improvement in job opportunities have led to many HNIs from corporate sector. We have to understand that rural Marketing is much different than its urban counterpart.

Diversity in Agricultural Seasons and Crops:

India is a very diverse country, having multiple climates in different parts, different crops and different crop patterns. The variation of temperatures in Northern region is 1 degree to 45 degree Celsius, whereas in south, it is almost stable around 30 degrees. The monsoon also varies and so does its arrival in the country leading to variation in crop patterns. The major crops in India are divided into four categories, Food Grains (Rice, Wheat, Maize, Millets and Pulses), Cash Crops (Cotton, Jute, Sugarcane, Tobacco, and Oilseeds), Plantation Crops (Tea, Coffee, Coconut and, Rubber) and Horticulture Crops (Fruits and Vegetables). On the basis of seasons, the crops in India have been divided into Rabi, Kharif and Zaid crops. These variations are the major causes of different challenges in different regions. The level of adoption of technology is also different in different regions. The fertiliser usage per acre in Arunachal Pradesh and Nagaland is 2.4 kg and 3.2 kg respectively whereas the usage in Haryana and Punjab is 220 kg and 243 kg. In most of the states in India, the average consumption is much below 200 kg per hectare. This vast variation also shows the huge opportunities in rural India, arable land vs non arable land and scope of micro irrigation and soluble agri inputs.

Uneven Level of Development in Rural India:

The variation in development level is clearly visible in the country. Even in the same state the level of infrastructural and other developments are at different levels. If we talk about the road infrastructure as of March 31, 2016, Maharashtra has the largest length of State Highway roads which is 33,705 km, whereas Uttar Pradesh, which is of almost similar size, has the State Highway road length of 8432 km. In the eastern part of India, the situation is much worse. Not only in road infrastructure but in the case of electricity supply as well, there is a huge difference in the development. Annual per capita consumption of electricity in Dadra & Nagar Haveli is 15783 whereas in Bihar it is 272. These factors are a real challenge to the marketers as the strategy required is different in different areas. Citing an example for vehicle campaigns, normally Tata Ace vehicle is used for branding at the village level. But due to lack of proper road infrastructure at the village level in MP, these vehicles do not work well and we need to use Mahindra Pickup, a stronger counterpart. However, Mahindra Pickup is much more expensive than the Tata Ace vehicle. Similar strategic variations are required at the ground level to handle activity in different regions. I will discuss about these in the Strategy part of the book.

Cultural Exchange Due to Internet Explosion:

Internet has helped the rural youth to connect with the global highway. Now they have access to almost any information in the world. They have access to the latest technology used in the world or in other states of India. Because of Internet, people are able to interact with each other from far off places and can share their views on any matter. The South Indian song *Kolaveri Di* had overnight become famous across India even though most people did not understand the lyrics of the song. I have seen many Punjabi singers becoming famous in non-Punjabi areas. This cultural exchange is not just a cultural exchange but a complete knowledge sharing and connection of the youth of India with each other leading to huge opportunities of growth as a country. There is a big community of *You Tubers* now a days. They are making videos on different topics in one region and have a following across India, even in deep rural pockets. This has inspired many to become You Tubers in rural areas as well. You can find many who have done a fairly decent job. Facebook connections, Instagram posts and now *Tik Tok* have changed the game. Ganesh Chaturthi is a big celebration in North India now, but was a very small affair some years back. South Indian and Gujrati food is available in the north and a North Indian thali is available in Chennai. Rural India is changing and it is changing fast. The youth are in blue denims with smart phones in their hands. Rural India is growing fast. Watch out marketers!

Growth of Middle Class in Rural India:

With the rise in employment opportunities in Tier III and IV cities, there is a growth in the educational and financial level of the rural people. Rural youth now have access to higher education and they have employment options near their homes. I have seen many agri graduates from Rural India and they have got decent jobs in Agri input industry near their homes in the rural heartland. Similar opportunities are created by banks, insurance sectors, hospitals, pharma companies, cement companies and many more. There is a middle class which is rising and who has exposure to the education as well as to the urban lifestyle. This class needs all sorts of facilities for themselves. They are fuelling the growth engine of India with their hard work and rising aspirations. The impact of these middle classes is huge on the rural mind-set. Rural India is now investing a lot on the education of their children for a better future. Many such educated youth have built enterprises of national repute from scratch and have changed fortunes. Fateh is one such company that started in the rural heartland of Punjab. It was started in a small town of Bathinda. More than 90% employees of Fateh are from rural India and many come from villages. The rise in rural economy have made this company bigger and now it has its headquarters in Mumbai, but its roots are rural. Thousands of companies like Fateh have grown in every small town of India and have fuelled the Indian economy. They have not only created jobs but ignited aspirations with dreams in the eyes of Rural Indians.

Growing Aspirations of Lower Classes:

With the rise in middle classes, there is a clear and visible change in the mind-sets of the lower classes. The people who did not own land and was working as labourers in agriculture or other areas have started learning skills and are now investing in education for their children. With the rise in mechanisation and automobile revolution because of easy financing a lot of skilled manpower is required. These classes are moving into the professions of electricians, mechanics, masons, plumbers, carpenters etc. and have improved the lives of many families in rural India. These professions are now becoming more important and many single skilled people are becoming self-employed and some with entrepreneurial mind-set have built small and big companies. As an example, there are many small mechanics of harvesters who became big industries over a period of time. Standard Tractors, Preet Tractors and even Sonalika is one of them. These aspirations and strength of people to fulfil their dreams is changing rural India. Young rural consumers aged 18 to 28, are extensively using digital technology and buying brands online to enhance their social image. They influence the decisions of other consumer segments in a big way. With the dreams in their eyes and the conviction in their attitude, with education and skills on hand, rural India is rising.

Rich Families without Landholding:

Employment opportunities have struck rural India in a big way. Many managerial and executive level jobs are created in different sectors working in these areas. These executives have huge urban influence. They are well educated and well versed with latest technologies and gadgets for better lifestyle. They are the potential customers for many brands. These companies are supported by a big vendor network. These vendors are entrepreneurs who provide products and services to these companies in rural areas. They have a lot of exposure to new things through these managers and executives who regularly interact and travel to the larger cities. There is a big and rich class of these managers, executives and vendors who need all sorts of facilities from big houses with all amenities from electrical to electronic gadgets like washing machine, smart TVs, branded cars, etc. They also understand the meaning of good education. They put their children in top private schools and use high end private medical facilities. They are also potential customers for the insurance companies and they are large in numbers. We can see a lot of Big Bazaars, Reliance retail stores, Best Price like wholesale and retail store chains in these areas. Even jewellery chains like Tanishq and Reliance Jewellers are opening up in these areas. Rural India is booming, go and grab your pie.

The rural market is, no doubt, a very lucrative market but it needs a lot of careful strategies. The diversity and the emergence of neo upper middle and middle classes have made this market much more important and challenging. With the advent of digital technologies, there are many opportunities available.

CHAPTER 4

Factors Influencing Rural Marketing

Rural marketing can be defined as fulfilling the aspirations of rural India, the aspirations of all classes, young and old, the educated, unskilled and the skilled, the women, farmers, labourers and every Indian residing in rural India. It fulfils their dreams, ambitions, and expectations from this country and the life they want. The influence of the cities, metros and foreign lands is entering their lives through TV and the internet. The girls are going to schools, colleges and universities. Women are becoming independent, running self-help groups, learning skills and holding strong and decisive positions in society. A lot of women sarpanches and corporate executives show the position is changing. The underprivileged society is rising with the power of skills and education, with the help of reservation and their hard work. The dream of social equality in India seems closer. With the rise in opportunities and financial support, MSME's are popping up everywhere with new and old ideas; performing, struggling, creating jobs, fulfilling dreams and giving vision to the society. The growth in the service sector white collared jobs in rural India have given birth to another class. The growth is apparent from the retail chains entering rural India. Government focussing on agriculture and allied sectors is a clear indication that the growth story of India will be written on the rural pages.

Rising Aspirations Of Rural India:

Rural India is aspiring for a better life and facilities with growth. They are aspiring for better education for their children, better employment opportunities, better infrastructural development, marketing solutions for their produce and products and conducive environment for business with best finance options. The change in the mind-set from a life of contentment to a life full of all facilities have changed the whole scenario in rural India. Rural Indians, after connecting with the mainstream media and internet, now want to enjoy all the luxuries which an urban Indian is enjoying. They have an aspiration to move into the malls, watch films in multiplexes, enjoy rides on Land Rovers, Mercedes and Audis. These aspirations are actually attracting the companies to reach them and provide them with solutions and opportunities for growth and a luxurious life. They are thinking of new ideas for processing their produce, building their companies and creating a niche in their profession. The aspirations are fuelling the ambitions giving birth to new ideas of making more money and building more resources. The growth story of Rural India is visible and have started taking the shape. The next few years will be different.

Urban Influence:

The rise of the Tier III and IV cities have given an insight into the urban life to rural India. These cities have become the business hub for the villages, where the buying and selling activity is happening. In these cities, rural India not only sells its produce but also buys every product of necessity. These cities have become the entertainment and marketing hubs. The malls and the multiplexes with variety of restaurants and restaurant chains like Pizza Hut, McDonalds, Sagar Ratna, etc. have changed the viewpoint of rural India. The malls have exposed them to all branded products like apparels, jewellery, electronic devices etc. Almost every household has a TV, a fridge and many have washing machines which is the direct impact of urban influence. These cities have given an opportunity to have wonderful education as number of CBSE and ICSE schools have started operating in these cities. With the rise of these cities, medical facilities have also improved with the entry of lot of private hospitals and labs. The banking systems have improved and many private banks have opened their branches in these cities. With the advent of these banking services, finance and insurance have become a big sector in these areas. The courier services reaching these cities have given access to many online E-commerce companies. The sales of these companies have increased multi fold in the rural India, thereby, impacting the lifestyle of rural India. Rural India is changing and need more and more services. Now is the time to reach the market and help them grow faster.

Women Empowerment:

Women are almost 50% of our population. Rise in education and employment opportunities, with government and social initiatives for women empowerment have started showing results. Now the girls are not forbidden from education in schools, rather in most of the families girls are getting equal opportunities for education in good schools and colleges. This change in the mind-set have made women much more confident and independent. This independence and awareness have made women much more decisive than earlier years. The employment opportunities have given women the power to show their talent and skills at their workplace. The working women in government and private offices have become influencers in the society. They decide about all household purchases. They also take responsibility to handle children and their needs, so the buying actually is done by women in these families. The political reservation for women seats in panchayat elections have also worked well towards women empowerment. The companies are working in this area to make their presence felt. Project Shakti by HUL connects with rural population by promoting women empowerment along with satisfaction of their distribution and penetration objectives. The rural India is witnessing more and more independent women with time and this segment of citizens cannot be neglected anymore.

The constitutional change which made women equal shareholders of the family property have given women much more power than any other initiative. But still society has not started this practice. Now women have started fighting for their rights. Hope to see that real equality comes in India in the coming years. I can see much more women entrepreneurs than yesteryears.

Social Equality and Reservation:

The menace of the caste system has been hitting the growth of India since ages. The constitutional empowerment of the socially backwards have started showing some results now. With the reservations in place and a lot of government and social initiatives, society has now started accepting the equality of all humans to some extent. Yet a lot has to be done in order to make the dream of Dr. Ambedkar come true. With many educational and job guarantee initiatives, there is some improvement in the lives of our lowest strata. But still more than

800 million people in India are considered poor. Most of them live in the countryside and keep afloat with odd jobs. 70% of our population is working hard to make ends meet and comes under extremely poor status. Two-thirds of people in India live in poverty, 68.8% of the Indian population live on less than $2 a day. Over 30% have less than $1.25 per day available. They are considered extremely poor. These classes need to be taken care of in order to make India progress the way we are dreaming. If 70% population improves its income by 10%, just imagine the kind of growth the economy is going to have. The entrepreneurship needs to be given better chance and only solution to these problems seem to be better education, better health services and better employment opportunities. Hope the Government of India is listening.

MSME Revolution:

The industries are the backbone of any economy. Quality employment opportunities and export income depends on the industrial strength of the country. In India, the base of industrialisation was strengthened when the public sector units were started. But when the economy was opened and the financial credit became easy, there was a spurt in the MSME sector. The medium and small scale industries got the boost with increase in demand in the domestic and export market. The manufacturing output of MSMEs was close to 30 trillion Indian rupees during the financial year 2015. The output accounted for a contribution of almost 31% to the GDP in 2015. The service sector alone had an employment figure of approximately 50 million, whereas the manufacturing sector could only pull off half that number. These employment opportunities generated by the MSMEs in Rural India have also helped to generate the demand in the market for products. Conducive atmosphere for the business will certainly improve the situation of employment leading to better market opportunities.

Service Sector Growth:

India's services sector covers a wide variety of activities such as trade, hotel and restaurants, transport, storage and communication, financing, insurance, real estate, business services, community, social and personal services, and services associated with construction. The service sector contributes 60% of the total GDP of India and employs around 25% of the total workforce. The growth of the service sector actually improved the lifestyles of the rural Indians. This sector has helped in improving the employment opportunities to women in Rural India. Now you can find a lot of females working in schools, banks and other offices in different positions. This has led to women empowerment as well as an increase in the family's income. Many highly qualified women got opportunities in these organisations. This sector is also responsible for the rise of the middle classes. These classes have changed the purchasing pattern of rural India.

Retail Chains, E-Commerce Sites and Food Chains:

The prosperity in rural India is very much clear from the fact that many retail chains like Walmart, Best Price, Reliance retail, Big Bazaar, etc. have entered the Tier II and III cities. These retail chains have multiple effects on the economy of rural India. First of all, they have created jobs in these areas. Secondly, they came with a lot of investment and many vendors got good amount of work. Thirdly, they have started supporting many local brands who get an opportunity to display their products leading to a direct impact on the rural economy. The food chains like Pizza Hut, McDonalds and others procure the materials from the local markets. These retail chains have also given rural India a chance to fulfil their aspirations of going to a big store and shop. These stores have also inspired the local business communities to try such ventures and as a result many local chains have popped up in a similar way. Jewellery chains like Tanishq have started schemes like monthly EMI or monthly savings for the people so that they can buy jewellery as and when required. These retail chains have changed the mind-sets of people with online home deliveries and better quality products with complete complaint handling and customer care. They have been acting like growth engines for the Indian economy.

Government Initiatives:

The Government of India has planned various initiatives to provide and improve the infrastructure in rural areas which can have a multiplier effect in increasing movement of goods, services and thereby improve the earning potential of rural areas subsequently improving consumption. The Government of India has approved the proposal to construct 10 million houses for the rural population, which will require an investment outlay of Rs. 81,975 crore (US$ 12.7 billion) for the period 2016–17 to 2018–19. The Government of India aims to provide tap water regularly to every household by 2030 in line with United Nations Sustainable Development Goals, requiring a funding of Rs. 23,000 crore (US$ 3.57 billion) each year until the target is met. The Government has introduced various reforms in the Union Budget 2017–18 to uplift the rural markets. Some of the key high-lights of the Budget are: Rs. 187,223 crore (US$ 28.08 billion) has been allocated towards rural, agriculture and allied sectors. The allocation for Pradhan Mantri Aawas Yojana Gramin has been increased from Rs. 15,000 crore (US$ 2.25 billion) to Rs. 23,000 crore (US$ 3.45 billion) in the year 2017–18 with a target to complete 10 million houses for the homeless by the year 2019. The pace of roads construction under Pradhan Mantri Gram Sadak Yojana (PMGSY) has been accelerated to 133 km per day as against an average of 73 km per day during the years 2011–14. The allocation to the Mahatma Gandhi National Rural Employment Guarantee Act (MGNREGA) has been Rs. 48,000 crore (US$ 7.2 billion) in the year 2017–18, which is the highest ever allocated amount. The Government of India is looking to install Wi-Fi hotspots at more than 1,000 gram panchayats across India, under its ambitious project called Digital Village, in order to provide internet connectivity for mass use, as well as to enable delivery of services like health and education in far-flung areas. In the Union Budget 2017–18, the Government of India mentioned that it is on course to achieve 100% village electrification by May 1, 2018. The Government of India has sought Parliament's approval for an additional expenditure of Rs. 59,978.29 crore (US$ 8.9 billion), which will be used to support the government's rural jobs scheme, building rural infrastructure, urban development and farm insurance.

CHAPTER 5

Government Initiatives

The growth of the nation depends on the prosperity of its citizens on the whole. The foundation of this prosperity is based on equality. The equality which is enshrined in our constitution is the basis of our prosperity and growth of our country. We, as the citizens and as a society, have to implement this constitutional principle in order to realise our dreams of making our country a developed nation. If we talk about Rural India and its economy, our dependence on agriculture is huge, here the role of the agriculture universities is quite commendable. These universities researched and gave new seeds and technologies to farmers. Many agricultural awareness programs were started to make new ways of agriculture famous. These universities made the green revolution possible and India became the net exporting country in food. Our leaders thought of the industrial economy. The advent of the Public Sector Units and then making those Navratnas fuelled the economy of the regions where they were set up. The agricultural development led to the installation of many fertiliser and agri input factories in deep rural parts of India. Developed clusters were formed around these economic ventures. The industrial development required literate and skilled people. Government's initiative of literacy campaigns and primary and secondary school networks did wonders. In the decade of 80–90, the advent of computers is impacting the economy now with the online processes and banking operations. The cooperative movements and public private partnership with opening of economy have created myriads of opportunities.

The government's focus on the health and the cleanliness drive in the name of Swach Bharat Abhiyan has improved the awareness about health and sanitation. The Skill India, Start-up India and many other such schemes have given birth to many social and rural start-ups. Now the Delhi government's model of health and education with the advent of mohalla clinics is discussed across the country. These initiative are making rural India more conducive to development.

The Constitution of India:

Article 14 of the Constitution of India states: "The State shall not deny to any person equality before the law or the equal protection of the laws within the territory of India." This law, if interpreted, also talks about equal opportunities to grow and right to living. The foundation of the development of our country is the Constitution of India. Our constitution has protected the nation as a whole from many highhandedness that happened in the past. We, as a society, must do our duty to make this constitution work and build a society where every person is equal. Rural development lies in equality. We, as a society, have to change and follow our constitution.

Role of Agricultural Universities:

The agricultural development has been the foundation of the rural development. Around 70% of our population depends on agriculture and allied professions alone. When we got independence, India was the net import country in food. With the awareness programs and technological innovations of agricultural universities, the growth in agriculture has been tremendous. The Green Revolution was the result of the efforts by the agriculture universities. Punjab Agricultural University, established in 1962, played a key role in ensuring India becomes self-sufficient by ringing in the Green Revolution. The awareness programs consist of the Krishi Vigyan Kendras (KVK), Seasonal Farmer Fairs by universities and KVKs. The extension programs are by department of agriculture of the state. This revolution has happened only in pockets and the whole of India has not benefitted from it. Now with the advent of private companies into the business, the overall development across the country has started. According to PAU's Vice Chancellor Baldev Singh Dhillon, "Agricultural needs have changed dramatically over the years. The challenge now is to strike the right balance between economic success and environmental conservation. Agriculture can no longer be about brute production."

Industrialisation and Navratna Effect:

The direct impact is mainly in terms of the demand for men and materials unit and the value added which is its contribution to the regional as well as national income. The indirect impact may further be classified into two categories, viz. Multiplier Effects and Propulsive Effects.

The multiplier effects occur in terms of the increased income of the direct beneficiaries of the unit. The propulsive effects of the units would be in terms of generation of activity in the industries linked to the public sector either as supplier of inputs or consumers of outputs.

Public and private sector enterprises like Tata, Birla and others have rendered useful help and service in the development of human resource in backward areas for changing the traditional character of village life. Investment in human capital is considered an essential ingredient of development planning. Such development is only possible if rural talents are identified properly fed with modern knowledge of relevant science and technology.

A large number of public sector undertakings have been set up in the backward areas/regions/districts in order to capitalise the rural labour by equipping them with vocational education, technical training and managerial skills. The strategy behind this is to transform the unemployed rural people to get self-motivated and self-inspired employment avenues in local economic activities. The government's support to private sector industrial units in the areas like Jamshedpur and others have helped the areas to develop.

Literacy Campaign:

"If I learn carpentry from an illiterate carpenter only I know, how to do work, but if I learn from a literate carpenter, my thoughts will be stimulated" – Mahatma Gandhi.

Government has taken many steps for higher literacy rate. Right to Education Act declares that all children up to the age of 14 are entitled to free compulsory education. Children are provided free education in the government schools. Moreover, the expenses of books and uniforms are also borne by the school for poor children. Mid-day meals are also provided to the children. Besides, there are many programs like Ladli that have been introduced to raise the enrolment and education of a girl child. Adult education is also taken up in many villages by the schools to spread awareness and literacy among illiterate adults. Some of the schemes are, Shiksha Sahayog Yojana, Sarva Shiksha Abhiyan, Saakshar Bharat, Kanya Saaksharta Protsahan Yojna, Kasturba Gandhi Balika Vidyalaya Yojna.

These schemes have worked well and today almost the entire country is literate.

Effect of Introduction of Computers:

Computers were introduced in India in the eighties with the help of many private computer education companies entering India. The impact of this policy can be easily gauged with the fact that today we have many conglomerates in software like Infosys, TCS and HCL. We have become a significant player in software technologies in the world. The impact on rural India is great because the banking sector has become completely online. The government websites provide information in all local languages and is a much easier way to propagate the information. Many e-commerce sites today working in Tier III and IV cities have been able to help the rural economy to grow. Weather forecast to crop cultivation and online trade have all been possible today because of this. All this has happened because of the government policy of introducing computers in India in those days.

Cooperative Movement:

The cooperative movement in India today is the largest in the world, with more than 6 lakh individual cooperatives covering sectors such as credit and banking, fertiliser, sugar, dairy, marketing, consumer goods, handloom, handicrafts, fisheries, tribal development, labour and housing catering to over 24 crore members. The total working capital base in the cooperative sector is estimated at about Rs. 73,000 crores. The dairy cooperative is another success story in India. The Anand model for cooperative milk marketing from Gujarat, with its well-recognised Amul brand, provided the blueprint for replicating its success elsewhere under the National Dairy Development Board program, contributing to the success of Operation Flood. In fertiliser production and distribution, the Indian Farmers Fertiliser Cooperative (IFFCO) controls over 35% of the market. In the production of sugar, the cooperative share of the market is 58% while in the marketing and distribution of cotton, it is 60%. Cooperative sector accounts for 55% of the production in the hand-woven textiles sector, whereas cooperative marketing and distribution channels account for 50% of the edible oil market in India. Dairy cooperatives in India, operating under the leadership of the National Dairy Development Board, collectively, are the largest producer of milk in the world. (Reference: Press Information Bureau, Government of India, Vice President's Secretariat, July 8, 2016)

Opening of Economy:

The economic liberalisation of the economic policies in India was initiated in 1991. It helped the economy become more market and service oriented and expanded the role of private and foreign investment. With this policy the private sector got a huge push and the ease of doing business became much better. Financing is a crucial component for economic development. Shedding light on this important area of rural economy, Manish Jaiswal, MD & CEO, Magma Housing Finance & SME Business said, "As a Non-Banking Financial Company (NBFC), we are operating across India with 300 branches. Out of 300 branches, 80% are located in the semi-urban and rural areas. Our tractor finance is doing better than housing and MSE financing. Direct Benefit Transfer (DBT) payments are being transferred to the beneficiaries by 4 crore electronic accounts.'

Public Private Partnership:

Since its inception in 1982, National Bank for Agriculture and Rural Development (NABARD) has played a crucial role in creating infrastructure in rural India. Highlighting its renewed impetus on water and irrigation, its Deputy Managing Director, HR Dave said, "We work with the states for creating rural infrastructure. Water has been recognised as a key driver of growth in the last year's budget under which a long time irrigation fund has been created in NABARD. For water use efficiency, a micro-irrigation fund has been created in which a lot of private companies are involved." Food processing sector's importance in providing remunerative prices to the farmers for their produce has led NABARD to give special impetus on funding food processing, agricultural warehousing and cold infrastructure. "Food processing and cold chain sectors are other key drivers of the rural economy. Thus, 20% of India's warehouses are funded by NABARD. APMCs (Agricultural Produce Market Committees) are being integrated with technology and modernised with funds from NABARD," Dave added.

Subsidy Schemes:

The Economic Times recently held its 5th edition of Rural Strategy Summit in New Delhi. The two day summit witnessed the large number of marketers, researchers, policy makers and advertising professionals, focused on India's rural markets. In his inaugural speech, Dr. Nagesh Singh, Additional Secretary, Union Ministry of Rural Development, highlighted the government's push for social sector schemes, leading to increasing rural incomes, rural infrastructure development and overall growing rural economy.

Rural Employment Generation Schemes:

Highlighting the crucial role of animal husbandry in the rural economy, the Managing Director of India's largest farmers' cooperative, Gujarat Cooperative Milk Marketing Federation (GCMMF), popularly known as AMUL, RS Sodhi said during addressing the Summit, "Despite housing 68% of India's population, rural India contributes only 46% to national income. Cultivation is contributing 32% to rural income while animal husbandry's contribution is 12% and wages and services contribute 56% to rural income generation. Animal husbandry is generating Rs. 500,000 crore through dairy only. Due to its crucial role, the sector needs to be given special focus." Many similar initiatives are taken by the government for rural employment like Skill India, MNREGA etc. which are impacting rural India's growth story.

Health Initiatives and Swachh Bharat Abhiyan:

Open defecation has been a major challenge in India. Thus, it has led the Government of India to run dedicated rural sanitation programmes. Earlier it was Nirmal Bharat Abhiyan (Total Sanitation Programme) and now it has been upgraded to form Swachh Bharat Abhiyan which has been providing funds for making toilets in rural India and making people aware of cleanliness. Speaking on the status of sanitation in rural India, Deepak Kumar Mitra, SATO (Safe Toilet) Business Head, South Asia, LIXIL Water Technology said, "More than 30% population in India do not have toilets and goes for open defecation." On the impact of digital communication in the hinterland, he said, "WhatsApp and Facebook have made huge impact in rural India, thus we have found them very effective media for reaching rural consumers. With education and penetration of digital media, rural consumers are being turning very demanding whether it is for goods or services, it is going to be very challenging for the marketers to meet their standards."

National Schemes on Entrepreneurship and Skill Development:

Multiple schemes for the entrepreneurship are developed by government. Schemes are meant for small to medium scale companies. The Skill India and Start-up India are the latest ones. You can logon to https://msme.gov.in/all-schemes for all the subsidy schemes for MSME sector including government schemes.

Delhi Model of Health and Education:

Although Delhi doesn't come under rural India but the model built by the Government of Delhi needs mention here. The rural population consists of 70% poor. So in order to give them good education, model schools like the State of Delhi should be developed in the rural areas in other states. The Delhi model of Mohalla clinics and the government hospital facilities are very low or no cost and commendable. These models should be replicated across the country. These models will certainly change Rural India's face and fate.

Road Ahead:

As is the trend with Urban India, consumers in the rural regions are also expected to embrace online purchases over time and drive consumption digitally. The rural regions are already well covered by basic telecommunication services and are now witnessing increasing penetration of computers and smartphones. Taking advantage of these developments, online portals are being viewed as key channels for companies trying to enter and establish themselves in the rural market. The Internet has become a cost-effective means for a company looking to overcome geographical barriers and broaden its reach. Market research firm Nielsen expects India's rural FMCG market to reach a size of US$ 100 billion by 2025. Another report by McKinsey Global Institute forecasts the annual real income per household in rural India to rise to 3.6% by 2025, from 2.8% in the last 20 years. Exchange Rate Used: INR 1 = US$ 0.0155 as on June 20, 2017. (References: Media Reports, Press Releases, Press Information Bureau (PIB), Accenture Report, Nielsen Report, Budget 2016–17).

CHAPTER 6

Rural Marketing Opportunities

Here in this chapter we will discuss about the opportunities in the coming 15 to 20 years in rural India. We, as a country, have developed in all aspects and still a lot needs to be done. Overall and as per various studies, development of rural power, irrigation, water, sanitation and road infrastructure can increase productivity, savings, income and tourism and result in better jobs and health of rural people. The infrastructural development includes roads, warehouses, irrigation, industry, markets, ports and export hubs. The health facilities for the country need a special boost as we are lagging behind in this especially where rural India is concerned. The new technologies in agriculture includes the regional weather forecasting, satellite based land analysis of the fertiliser utilisation, pest and disease attacks on the crops. We also need to work on the crop yields improvement with lesser usage of water and other resources. The marketing and processing of these crops need a special focus. Education is another field where we need a lot of development. Education need to be redesigned for the practical utilisation of knowledge in every field. Upgrading of the information in education is the dire need. The use of digital media is certainly going to increase in every aspect of life, the question is how best we could use it and how best we could make our lives out of it, as a country how we could connect the local markets with the global ones. China has achieved a lot in the last three decades. The important question is, can we do it in the next two decades? Agriculture also needs machines and they need to be India centric. We need more agro-mechanisation and automation in the coming years. There are many other aspects which could be discussed but the major points we will discuss are given below. Hope I will be successful in portraying a clearer picture of future of India in this chapter.

Scope of Infrastructural Development:

There are around 6 lac villages in India. All the villages are economic hubs which are connected to the nearby small and big towns. They are the primary producers of food and many other articles. The kuccha roads cover a large portion of the rural road network in entirety, which are highly vulnerable and inaccessible particularly during the rainy season. Given the wide diversity in physical structure of the country, the need for greater surfaced road connectivity is particularly important in the hilly terrains and low lying areas. They need infrastructure for the quick transportation of their products to the place of need. The monsoon irregularity always create havoc in the lives of the farmers, resulting in a dip in economy of the country. The irrigation innovation is required at all levels. The irrigation projects are required and should be designed in such a way that every village gets a canal water for drinking and irrigation. They need technologies to reduce the flood irrigation methods and the need to produce more crop per drop. Although some measures are taken by governments by subsidising the micro irrigation equipment, a lot more is required to grow at a faster pace. They need state of the art warehouses where they could store the produce for longer periods of time. They need marketing infrastructure connected through digital technologies. The processing plants near these villages would develop a lot of economic activity around them, leading to economic abundance and growth. They can get optimum prices and the value for their products by these measures. These villages contain artisans as well who are always robbed by the middlemen who pose as helpers to them many times in the form of NGOs and other agencies. They need to be connected directly to the market across the world so that they may sell their products directly. Hope techno entrepreneurs of India sitting in Bengaluru, Pune and Hyderabad are listening. The export houses, the ports and the airports need to be connected directly to these villages and small towns for their growth. All this is going to happen in the next 20 years, the growth in rural India is going to be amazing and as marketers we have a lot to accomplish.

Electricity has become a necessity for every household. The governments at the Centre and States have been trying to push various reforms in power sector in order to provide electricity to people at affordable prices. However, even within the electrified villages, many households are not connected with electricity. Adequate electric supply is feasible only with the public private partnership where the government could regulate the rules and electricity fares and the production and distribution can be done by the private players. Secondly the alternate methods of generating electricity like solar, wind and hydro power should be promoted on village levels. Every village can be self-sufficient in electricity through this model at least for the basic needs. This infrastructural costs could be borne either by the governments or through long tenure loans at very low interests to the village or a combination of both. This sector could boost the economy at a large scale.

Health Facilities Development:

Health of the citizens of the country shows its prosperity level. The health facilities in rural India are in a pathetic shape. As on March 2011, a total of 6.4 lac villages in the country were covered with only 23,887 Primary Health Centres (PHCs) and 1,48,124 Sub-Centres. This shows that on an average 4.3 villages have one sub-centre and only one PHC exists for as many as 27 villages. Added to this, many health centres are also running without doctors (or absentee doctors) and in some cases treatment is done by unskilled healthcare workers. Absence of connectivity to the villages and inadequate number of health centres and skilled health workers still endangers the life of rural population in the country. There is requirement for clinics, hospitals and testing labs at every taluka level and even in villages. The clinics should be there in every village. There are some medical practitioners in villages but most of them are not adequately qualified. There are some private hospitals and doctors practising individually at some small towns as well but the ratio is very less and they are quite expensive. Here in this sector some low cost innovations by the private sector is required. The government's role is crucial in this sector as the development of the villages is not possible without proper medical facilities in these areas. There is a huge scope of development in rural India in these areas.

I expect an exponential growth in this field in the next few decades. The chain of testing labs which have reached till Tier III will certainly reach Tier IV and to the villages in the coming years. The qualified staff from local areas would get the jobs and it will create huge opportunities for insurance and medicine. The government could connect medical insurance with private hospitals. The insurance at lower rates can be offered at rural areas and the hospitals in those local areas should be given incentives to operate from there. The insurance cover will allow the rural people to go to hospitals without feeling the financial burden and the private hospitals will be able to treat them through insurance companies. Here lies a huge business for medical insurance companies and the medical fraternity. These areas can be a booming market for pharmaceutical sector for the next 20 years.

Provisioning of safe drinking water to every household should be one of the basic policy priorities. However, Census 2011 reports a mere 30 percent of rural area being covered with tapped water supply. Households in the remaining rural areas in the country depend on other means like hand pumps, bore well and fetching water from nearby rivers and canals etc. The poor sanitation facilities in the rural belt have been an equally challenging issue for the government. These areas need an immediate attention.

Agricultural Development in the next 15 years:

Agriculture is the backbone of the Indian economy. Agriculture is the main livelihood in India's villages and consequently, not only does it employ over 50% of the population, but also makes up for 18% of the GDP. Growth in agriculture is going to come in multiple segments. There are technologies in seeds production, micro-organism based products for plants, satellite based solutions, sensors for multiple tests, reports and alerts. There are also disease controlling methodology, irrigation technologies and mechanical automations to reduce the labour intensiveness and agricultural effectiveness. The new technologies by using digital, microbiology and satellite technology is going to change the agricultural world completely in the coming years. The growth in agriculture and its allied services will be huge and there is going to be a big scope for marketing with the rise in income levels of rural India. But the variation and new innovations will be required by the marketers as well. The mapping of every land with the help of the satellites would help the companies to provide the solutions to the farmers on an individual basis. Even governments would be able to provide alerts and other scheme related information to the farmers directly on this basis. The coming years will be years of transformation.

Educational Development:

The role of education is to improve the intellectual level of the students so that they may become good citizens and make their living through their passion and live wonderful and fulfilling lives. In India, most of the education is focussed on building the workforce and is blocking the minds of students to think outside the box. There is a dire need to change the pattern of the education system in order to convert thoughts into reality. Education is mostly focused towards the urban economy and it does not focus on the rural economy and neither are we inculcating the rural problems in the curriculum. There is a need to focus on rural India and the need to think about the problems they are facing. Then and only then the people of India after coming out of schools will start thinking about its solutions. We also need the schools to have open debates about the solutions that can be provided to the society. Such models should be built and they should be supported by the industry in order to convert them into reality. The interaction with the industry and entrepreneurs should be increased instead of bureaucrat interaction. Mostly in the school annual days the public servants are called as chief guests leading to the servant mind-set of the students instead of the freedom of thought. For that we need to connect with the entrepreneurs. Even the colleges and the universities should have at least one entrepreneur on the board for the guiding the students. Of course we need more schools and better education. But some change is visible as the private sector is the major source of the jobs, now some management and professional universities have started calling corporates but still the entrepreneur mind-set is lacking. But I believe this will change in the coming years. Rural India's growth lies in the hands of rural entrepreneurs not bureaucrats.

Digital Media and AI Development:

The rise in digital media and its changing face in the next 15 years will be with the help of technologies like AI, satellites and many more yet to present. The smartphone revolution will see a next level of interaction of what companies will be doing with the customers. The satellites will be mapping every inch of the land and even count the cattle every farmer has in his household. These demographic revolutions with the help of technology will certainly help in reducing the farming cost and will also help in reducing the input resource utilisation. The efforts on lesser water and fertiliser usage has already started and will be a reality in the coming years. These changes will certainly need another level of variation in the rural marketing. The companies need to change their strategy to move to digital to improve their digital footprint on a war level if they want to be in the race. The coming years are the years of technology. Although the human connection will always be there, need to reduce the human effect will be the key.

Local Markets Connecting with Global Markets:

There was a time when a village was having an independent economic system. Later the village was connected to the towns and the interdependence was established but now is the need to connect these economies to the world economy directly. We need the export hubs at the regional levels and we need transportation direct to the ports from these hubs. The ecosystem should be developed so that farmers understand the requirement of the world and they produce and process to export and get better value for their produce. The artisans, the entrepreneurs at these levels should be given special trainings and support in order to connect with the world economies. The education system should be complementing the skills we already have. These initiatives have started in some areas and will speed up with time and we expect the rural economy to be booming in the next 10 years. The marketers need to be closely watching the changes happening in these areas.

Agri Processing and Export Houses:

Agricultural produce which we are exporting in raw form is the major cause of the farmer distress and lower value creation of the product. We need to focus on the processing plants in every part of the country with the multiple crops and the small setups being handled by farmers themselves or by the big industries in the vicinity. This will not only improve the marketing activity near the villages but also create more jobs in that area. These initiatives have started. We could see a lot of wine making distilleries in western Maharashtra which have helped grape farmers to flourish. I believe more such initiatives can do wonders if the government supports them with policy framework.

Agro Mechanisation and Automation of Rural India:

The mechanisation in agri-sector have been on the rise since many decades. But now with the integration of communication channels and availability of knowledge and awareness, it has become seamless. This activity has helped the farmers to adopt new technologies into their lifestyle and farming. Many automation companies and auto mechanisation have entered into the market and are making solutions available. This market is going to improve a lot in the coming years. The integration of automation with internet and connecting it with satellites would be doing wonders. I believe the next few decades will be completely different. I expect there will be huge changes in marketing as well.

STRATEGIES

CHAPTER 7

Identification of Customers

The most challenging part of the rural market is that there are pyramids within the pyramids. The rural market is quite complex as far as the consumers are concerned and identifying the right prospect is the real game winning formula. The identification of the consumers can be on the basis of the land holding. But the crop patterns play a very vital role. The cash crop areas do have much more purchasing power than the field crop or conventional agricultural areas. The awareness and knowledge levels also play an important part. There are industrial hubs in the rural areas where the purchasing power automatically improves with the employment opportunities available there. The educationally developed areas are more aware of the brands. The women empowerment is one of the major reasons for rural growth. The internet explosion and the role of mass media, especially vernacular papers and magazines, have a big role in changing the mind-set so studying that is very important before identifying the prospects. The type of product and the service is, of course, an important part. Mostly, major part of the rural market holds a very divergent pattern of reacting to marketing. So, the marketer needs to design a specific marketing mix for the rural segments. For rural market, a marketing manager has three options – first is to design a marketing programme common for all types of customers; the second is to design a marketing programme purely for rural customers and the third is to design a marketing programme for customers residing in rural but reacting as if they were global.

Identification on Land Holding Basis:

Land holding is one of the major basis for identification of the customers in the rural market. In every village, 70% land is owned by 30% of the families. These 30% farmers or families contain well educated members, these families have maximum impact of urbanisation. They like to have all the luxuries in their lives and even follow the global patterns. They send their children to the best schools in the area or many put them in the best schools of India. These families have substantial influence over the political activities of the area as well. They have much more resources than even urban higher middle class. These families own big agro machinery, best tractors, luxury cars and big houses. They are targeted by all luxury brands in all segments. The women in these families are also well educated and are aware of the latest trends and go for shopping for best apparels, jewellery and other accessories.

The other 70% of these rural population follow these families and try to imitate them. But with their economic conditions they have to satisfy their ego with the lesser brands. The small sachet sales by the big brands in FMCG have worked wonders for them as they were able to buy them. The sales of the beauty creams in these areas clearly shows the increasing awareness and consciousness about beauty in these areas. These families with small land holdings are trying to use innovations in agriculture and the landless are trying to get jobs in nearby towns after education. The identification of these customers on the basis of land is useful for the agro input industry, luxury brands, apparels, insurance companies, tractor and automobile industry and many more.

Crop Patterns in the Region:

The crop patterns are one of the most important way of identifying the customers. There are conventional crops which are normally done by the farmers with large land holdings, whereas, the cash crops like vegetables or fruits are done mostly by the marginal or small farmers. But the cash crops like vegetables, chilli or tomatoes are high yielding and give good earnings for these farmers due to which they are able to live a good lifestyle. The crop patterns and the area where these crops are sown is also very important as normally due to the regular year round activity because of these crops the employment opportunities in the form of labour, transportation and even small industries like tomato paste companies. The markets near these areas are also booming because of the trading activity happening on a regular basis. The identification on the basis of the crop patterns can be very useful for the companies like FMCG, food products, electrical home appliances, etc.

Awareness Levels about a Particular Utility:

They respond to those products that suit their religious faith and social norms and customs. They ask for such products which can assist in their traditional occupations and life style. They have minimum urge for individuality. They prefer family-used products than personal used products. They strongly prefer such products that can change and improve their life-style. They are less concerned with product services associated with products like after-sales services, guarantee and warranty, home delivery, and other similar services. Branding, packaging and labelling have less influence compared to urban segments, but it depends from product to product. But in some areas and some segments of customers do need proper warranty and services as in the case of automobiles or agro mechanical devices, etc. Even the service sector or the information based services also work well, for example, the RML service of information is sold at a good price to grape farmers. In this service, they provide the weather services, mandi rates and other related information. The utility is also an important aspect to identify the target segment.

Impact of Industrial Corridors:

The industrial corridors in the rural belts of India have played an important part in the growth of rural India. Besides the employment generation, a lot of entrepreneurial activities have also been initiated. Banks, cinemas, markets and many brands have entered those areas because of these corridors. The consumption of many items like milk, vegetables and other necessary items have gone up substantially leading to increase in income of many households. The automobile sales and the maintenance needs have improved, there is the need of all the skilled work force like plumbers, painters, carpenters, etc. All these have actually worked well for the rural markets to grow. Marketers need altogether a different strategy for these areas.

Educational & Employment Opportunities for Women:

With the initiation of various rural development programmes and agricultural development, there has been an upsurge of employment opportunities for the young educated rural youth. One of the biggest cause behind the steady growth of the rural market is that it is not exploited and also yet to be explored. The rural customer today is very aware and well educated and well versed with new ideas and new technologies but the level of education and awareness varies. They vary significantly in terms of preferences and habits. They are to be treated in different patterns. There are families with low land holdings but these families now have understood that if they want to live the lifestyle of the upper class of rural India then they have to educate their children. General education and even education for women have improved a lot in rural India. Now with the opening of the service sector, many jobs for women are opening up. Banks, insurance companies, automobile showrooms, call centres, administrative and clerical jobs and reception jobs are all available for the girls. Even the medical centres and private hospitals have huge opportunities for the girls to work as doctors and nurses.

Studying Cultural and Social Habits:

We find different types of buyers in rural areas. Some are simple, while some are sophisticated; some are extreme rich, while some are extreme poor; some are highly educated, while some are completely illiterate; some are dynamic and modern, while some are very rigid and orthodox; some believe in quality and status, while some believe in availability and price. Rural customers are gradually transforming into urban, metropolitan and even cosmopolitan customers. Improved education, rapid means of transportation, access to advance communication, raised living standards, craze to follow modern (even ultramodern) life pattern and many similar factors have drastically changed rural consumer behaviour. The gap between urban and rural segments tend to be notably narrow. Sometimes, rural and urban customers exhibit no difference at all. The social status of the rural regions is precarious (uncertain) as the income level and literacy varies extremely along with the range of traditional values and superstitious beliefs that have always been a major impediment (obstacle) in the progression of this sector. Hence, there exist various types of buyers with varied responses to products. Change in the joint families to the nuclear families have also helped to improve the demand.

Impact of Promotion on the Rural Customer:

Rural customers are highly attracted by local and regional promotional efforts. Their reference groups consist of educated and non-educated family members and relatives living in urban areas and foreign countries as well. Personal selling seems more influential to convince rural mass. They are attracted by such sales promotional tools or articles which are useful in their routine life such as knife, gas lighter, rings, key-chains, caps, photos of local actors, calendars and cards with religious impression, etc. They have a strong faith in local religious and spiritual leaders. Such leaders are among the most influential reference groups. Publicity efforts related to local vocational and agricultural activities can impress them. They can be appealed by visual or pictorial advertisements published in local and regional languages.

Role of Product or Service:

Rural consumers go to their nearest cities when they have to buy products like tractors, televisions, motorcycles, etc. Rural consumers go to the 'local market' which is normally around 5–10 km from their villages to buy the daily household requirements like sugar, tea, vegetable oil, etc. The rural market in India is vast and scattered and offers a plethora of opportunities in comparison to the urban sector. It covers the maximum population and regions and, thereby, the maximum number of consumers. Rural markets (buyers) believe in product utility as well as status and prestige. However, they like novel products with distinctive features. Most village customers consider tastes rather than usefulness in the long run. They like simple and long life products. They are interested in immediate results. Products must offer immediate benefits. Normally, they buy from familiar retailers and salesmen. They are hesitant to buy from big shopping malls or departmental stores. However, situation is changing gradually. Rural customers strongly favour relations. They continue buying from known and established retailers who maintain close family relations with them. Mostly, they buy from retail outlets situated in rural or sub-urban areas. However, some rural customers like to buy products from nearby cities also. Normally they place weekly to monthly orders as they don't want to come to the city frequently. They want immediate possession. They lack patience. They are found eager to possess and use the products immediately. Caste, religion, political party, relations, etc., play an important role in selecting the retailers. Online and direct marketing are not so much popular in rural areas. Sometimes, a few of them are interested in network marketing.

CHAPTER 8

Determining the Prices

"The moment you make a mistake in pricing, you're eating into your reputation or your profits."

– Katharine Paine

First and foremost you need to be financially informed. Before you set your pricing, work out the costs involved in running your business. These include your fixed costs (the expenses that will come in every month regardless of sales) and your direct costs (the expenses you incur by producing and delivering your products and services). Consequently, in case of rural marketing, the marketing mix has changed from the traditional '4 Ps' to the new '4 As,' i.e., affordability, awareness, availability and acceptability. A rural customer is price-sensitive mainly because of his relatively low level of income and unit price of a product will have an impact on sales. Pricing the product at a lower price really attracts rural population to try the products. This might be the general notion about rural market, but there are multiple segments in the rural itself; the high income class who owns land, the middle class with jobs and education and the lower income group. So selecting the target certainly helps us to determine the prices. The product's ability to solve a severe and urgent problem certainly gives it an edge as compared to a product that is required on a less urgent basis can also be a criteria for determining the prices. The market competitiveness, of course, is one of the factors and the brand positioning in the market is another. The advertising and marketing support certainly helps to build the brands and make it more pricey preposition. Nothing can cause confusion and doubt in a business like pricing your products and services. While you don't want to charge less than you are worth, you also don't want to price yourself out of the market, so how do you know if your price is right? Whether you are starting out or starting over, here are the factors to consider when pricing your products and services.

Selecting the Target Segment:

Know what your customers want from your products and services. Are they driven by the cheapest price or by the value they receive? What part does price play in their purchase decision? Also, look at what you are selling, are your current customers buying high-end or low-end products and services? This information will help you determine if your price is right, what level of services or inclusions you should be offering and lastly if you are targeting the right market. It may be that you need to change your market to make your business more profitable. There are super rich, although small in number, whose children study in most expensive schools and they go for very high quality products and price does not matter to them. There are minimum 3 to 4 families in every village. Some prefer credit facility. They normally have a strong desire to postpone payment for a certain period. Some middle class rural customers are attracted by instalment and loan facilities. The decision to cater to a particular segment is most important while deciding on the price.

Level of Problem Solved:

Business is getting a value for solving the problems. The more you solve the problems, the more you get value. Similarly the level of problem solved is also an important aspect. If you are solving a critical problem and solving an urgent problem, then certainly you will be valued higher than the lesser critical solutions. Similarly, if you take an example of the seed, then the highest yielding variety or hybrid will certainly fetch much more price than the other varieties. Similarly the business which solves the problems continuously will certainly fetch much more value.

Market Competition:

This is one of the few times you can give yourself permission to do a little competitor snooping. You might want to find out what they are charging for different products and services, what inclusions and level of service they are offering for those prices, what customers they are attracting with their pricing and how they are positioned in the marketplace. The answers to these questions will give you an industry benchmark for your pricing.

Brand Positioning:

Once you understand your customer, you need to look at your positioning. Where do you want to be in the marketplace? Do you want to be the most expensive, luxurious, high-end brand in your industry, the cheapest, beat it by 10% brand or somewhere in the middle? Once you have decided, you will start to get an idea of your ideal pricing.

Profitability:

One of the most important questions business owners neglect to ask themselves is, "How much profit do I want to make?" They tend to look at what others charge and then pull a figure out of the air to be competitive without giving consideration to how much profit they want and need. While you may be in the business for the passion and to add value to the lives of others, you also need to add value to your own. So give careful consideration to what your time is worth.

Advertising and Marketing Support:

The rural market in India is vast and scattered and offers a plethora of opportunities in comparison to the urban sector. It covers the maximum population and regions and, thereby, the maximum number of consumers. Rural market accounts for about 74% of the total Indian population. The social status of the rural regions is precarious (uncertain) as in some areas income level and literacy is extremely low along with the range of traditional values and superstitious beliefs that have always been a major impediment (obstacle) in the progression of this sector. They are easily attracted by price discounts and rebates. The advertising and marketing support will certainly take your product to masses and sales can be improved. The improved sales give you an edge for giving more schemes like that.

Pricing can be a difficult preposition but careful surveys of the market, selecting proper customer segment and understanding the problem it is going to solve is certainly going to help you.

CHAPTER 9

Marketing Communication

Marketing communication is the collective term for all the communication functions used in marketing a product, explaining its qualities and utilities for the customer. Marketing communication is one of the major elements of the four 'P's of marketing literature and is popularly termed as 'Promotion.' With the help of marketing communication, marketers attempt to inform, persuade, incite and remind consumers, directly or indirectly about their marketing offers. Marketing communication acts as a spokesperson of the brand and starts interacting with consumers on behalf of the company. In these ways, marketing communication allows marketers to transcend the physical nature of their products or the technical specifications of their services to imbue products and services with additional meaning and value. Marketing communication plays an important role in building and maintaining customer relationships and in leveraging these relationships in terms of brand and channel equity. The marketing communication depends on the type of the product and the service you want to promote. The communication should highlight the USPs and an attractive tagline which should connect to the consumer segment we want to focus on. The impact of culture and the role of vernaculars is a very critical part of the marketing communication. Choosing proper colours and signing the right celebrity is always a challenge. Although our country is highly diverse but the communication homogeneity is still required to build the brand.

Type of Product or Service:

The communication should focus on building relationships with the rural customers. This can be done by advertising for social causes prevalent in the rural areas like increasing awareness of the need for primary education while advertising for stationery products for education, communication through community development activities like promoting low cost water purifiers after setting up a tube well in a locality. It is essential to make the rural customers believe that the marketers consider them as valuable customers as they do for their urban counterparts. Project Shakti by HUL connects with rural population by promoting women empowerment along with satisfaction of their distribution and penetration objectives. ITC e-choupal connects with the farmers by considering them as business partners. Many companies even adopt villages for the development and this also leads to better understanding and positioning of the brands. Communications mix describes the range of approaches and expressions of a marketing idea developed with the hope that it will be effective in conveying the ideas to the target audience. The traditional media with its effective reach, powerful input and personalised communication system will help in realising the goal. Besides this, when the advertisement is couched in entertainment, it goes down easily with the rural consumers. Even the language and content must be according to the suitability of the rural environment. The Indian society is a complex social system with different castes, classes, creeds and tribes. The high rate of illiteracy, added to the inadequacy of mass media, impedes reach to almost 80% of India's population who resides in villages. Mass media is too glamorous, interpersonal and unreliable in contrast with the familiar performance of traditional artist whom the villager could not only see and hear but touch as well. Traditional media can be used to reach these people in the marketing a new concept.

Unique Selling Proposition (USP) Highlighting and Tagline:

The two vital arms of rural communication are the development of creatives to suit specific target audiences and communication delivery using appropriate vehicles. The role of the tagline and the USP is very important. The tagline, in a few words, clearly demonstrates the major utility of the product. Normally tagline consists of 3 to 4 words. Multiple colours and different font sizes are used to highlight the tagline. The tagline normally is written below the brand name and is the most visible communication in the image or the last slide of the video. The USP is the uniqueness of the product. Normally 2 to 3 USPs are highlighted in the communication. The USP is written after the tagline. These are very neat and clear which hits the consumer's mind. The communication flow is also very important. Though rural folks receive all types of selling messages through multiple sources, it has been found that the two tier system opinion leaders and the masses continue to exist. Opinion leaders continue to play an important role in the decision making, which is still community or group-based. However, the composition of the opinion leaders has changed over a period of time. For decisions regarding farm inputs, farmers may consult the traditional opinion leaders, including other successful farmers, agricultural officers and dealers. But with the growing aspiration levels (thanks to television), village youth who go to the cities for education and employment have also become important opinion leaders for lifestyle products. And in the case of personal care products, similar to the trend in the urban areas, school-going children do influence the brand decision.

Cultural Impact:

Companies are developing innovative strategies that break through the clutter and grab viewers' attention. Some of the unconventional advertising categories are: bus panel advertising and stall advertising. This area is changing constantly in the pursuit to find new ways to break through the advertising clutter. Consequently, more and more forms of unconventional advertising are identified by the economic literature. However, many of them are not applicable to the rural India context. With respect to communication channels, it has been found that when given a choice, individuals tend to perceive the oral channel as more efficient than the written channel when attempting to satisfy interpersonal needs. In addition, perceptions of friend's knowledge influenced an individual's assessments of their own knowledge which, influenced information search. Despite India's strides in many areas of technology, poor communications, especially in the rural areas, continues to hold back development. We at Fateh Rural Pvt Ltd (www.fatehrural.com) also started the call centre activity for many brands in rural India in agrochemical segment. But the call centres have to be in regional language based in Tier II or III cities. Call centres have helped in connecting directly with consumers and help saving their problems which at the next level will help to establish the brand. With the emergence in mobile telephony and 4G network and the development of social media like WhatsApp and Facebook, it has become easier to reach out and communicate with the rural areas although the impact as yet is very low.

Careful Vernacular Translations:

An effective way to increase the emotional attachment with rural consumers is the use of local language in the communication designed for a specific target group. This increases the involvement of the consumers with the brand. Moreover, the promotions should be designed with local concepts and practices so that the consumers can relate them with their day to day lives. Rural communication and the advertisement script should be such that it connects with that region where this advertisement is going to be released and shooting should also be done separately region wise. For example, the advertisement made for Telugu customers cannot be just dubbed and shown in northern parts of the country. We have to make another advertisement for that part for real effectiveness. Still in order to maintain the homogeneity, we need to translate. The translations should be done very carefully so that the real meaning of the communication should not change. Sometimes, a small spelling mistake can be fatal. Careful handling of the vernacular communication is a must and should be done by professional agencies only.

Colour Association with Brand:

The rural area is a market where large portions of the population are connected deeply with the culture and like deep colours. So, when packaging consumer products for rural markets, companies must use prominent logo symbols and logo colours to ensure that the consumers will be able to recognise the products. By creating a bond with the consumer through packaging, companies are able to establish a relationship that encourages repeat purchases. Loud, bright colours are typically used on packages to differentiate a product from another on the shelf and to create a lasting impression in the consumer's mind. Another technique used by multinational corporations has been tailoring products, including changing brand names to give them a rural image. In the eyes of the consumer, branded products are associated with quality and value. Therefore, communicating brand values through the package rather than with words becomes essential.

Monsanto used Bollgard as a name and magenta colour for the branding of BT technology in Cotton Seed, creating a brand with more than 90% share in their category.

Brand Ambassador Selection:

Companies will do well to use regional stars for regional campaigns for more effective penetration of brands in rural areas. The use of the local or vernacular film industry will work wonderfully well if you want to influence the rural consumer. The Punjabi film industry, Bhojpuri industry, the South Indian industry which works in Tamil, Telugu, Kannada and Malyalam can be much more effective than the Bollywood stars for these regions. Even in Marathi and Gujrati areas, there are many TV stars who can be much more effective and comparatively cheaper as well.

Homogeneity in Diversity:

Media reach in rural parts of India is very limited. Rural India consists of about 127 million households of which only 54% come in contact with any of the conventional media. The existing media-mix for reaching out to the consumers in rural needs improvement. Various problems prevailing in rural areas like low literacy, traditional bent of mind, inaccessibility to different media necessitate the adoption of a different approach for reaching out to them. Few companies have customised their rural advertising but still the outcomes are far less that those expected. The homogeneity in diversity is quite challenging. One communication across the country will not work. Rather multiple communications in each language have to be developed for a deep impact in the rural markets. Just like the crux of all the communications have to be the same, similarly, some major brand colours should also be the same. But the minute changes as per the culture and twist in the language as per the local dialect is, of course, required for the emotional connect with the customer. Different videos should be made region wise. The dubbed videos will have a diminished impact in rural India.

Focused Communication for Rural India:

Communication is your ticket to success, if you learn to do it effectively. It is important to understand the rural consumer to get your message across to him. Over the last 25 years, we have been involved in developing campaigns for a variety of products ranging from agri-inputs such as fertilisers, agro chemicals and seeds, to consumer durables, fast moving consumer goods and the services sector. This has helped us understand the special characteristics of the rural audience. A rural consumer may be illiterate according to the census definition, but he is very clever and blessed with a lot of common sense. He is highly conscious of value for money. There is a high involvement of the rural customer in any product purchase, more so for high-end products, which involve shelling out a few thousand rupees or more. Tricky, clever, gimmicky or even suggestive advertising does not work with the rural audience. 'Slice of life' approaches, simple and direct, using aspirational urban looking models work very well. Combining education with entertainment or 'edutainment' is a good route to take.

Companies will do well to use regional stars for regional campaigns for more effective penetration of brands in rural areas. In case of television spots which are sophisticated in execution, chances of the message going over the heads of the rural consumers is high. Therefore, special efforts will have to be made to interpret the main message to the rural audience. This could be done through a whole lot of below-the-line (BTL) activities, including road shows and VOW (video on wheels) programmes, which elaborate on the theme of the campaign through interactive games and contests. It is clear that in any form of rural communication, while we may have a national strategy, we have to think and act locally. An integrated package consisting of mass media and below-the-line activities works well.

CHAPTER 10

Advertising Campaigns and Strategies

"Advertising campaigns are devised to implement the marketing strategies and converting them into the real sales."

The advertising campaigns can be devised by taking many factors into account like the type of product, the target customer, the influencers, area of operation, mass media selection and the target's exposure to digital media. The life cycle of the product is also taken into consideration because the campaign will be different for new products as compared to established products whereby the strategy developed will be entirely different. The expansion to different areas is also a major challenge while developing a campaign. Multiple strategies are used by the rural marketers. Here, we will discuss about various types of campaigns which may be of some use to the marketers. Customer meets are done to showcase the product on first hand basis in order to build the brand. Multiple types of customer meets can be done. Companies can participate in local melas and exhibitions to register their presence. The weekly local markets (also called Haat Bazaars) and grain markets can also be an interesting place to use for marketing activities. Some companies use door to door campaigns and some identify the influencers and use them like their ambassadors of brands. TV, radio and newspaper advertisement can also be used for reaching out to masses in a particular area. But the most effective campaign could be the 360 degree campaign where the return on investment could be the best.

The strategies can be many but let's discuss about the most effective ones.

Customer Meets:

The most effective rural campaigns have been the one to one campaigns and these are accomplished in many ways.

The first one is meeting the customer in his village. During these customer meets, the advertisers use manpower to have regular customer meets in the area with assistance from the local dealers. A customer meet is designed in such a way that the customer is influenced through visuals using some branding materials like back banners, canopies, standees, take away leaflets.

During the branding, the homogeneous format is used in all the meets to establish the brand identity. A public address system is used for the audio explanation of the product. The interactive session is done in order to explain the product to the customer and even one to one session is done with the immediate prospects. Sometimes, even branded vehicles are used in such cases. Also, LED TVs or projectors are used by the promoters for films, interactive games and other such interactive activities to establish the brand. The promoter is trained for the pitch which is carefully designed in order to explain the product effectively to the customer.

The data of the interested prospects is collected and sent to the sales team or call centre for further follow-up which, if done effectively, will lead to sales in a big way.

These types of campaigns are mostly done by the agro input companies.

As the digital campaigns are integrated with the outdoor campaigns, the farmers could be connected to the Facebook page by requesting them to like it. Even the leaflets distributed could have a QR code connected with the campaign. The farmers can scan it and can connect with the Company's pages and campaigns for further engagement. Even webinars for multiple farmer meetings can be arranged by the company using experts through webinar digital technology.

Exhibition and Mela (Farmer and Religious Fairs) Participations:

A lot of fairs are organised in rural India. There are farmer fairs, religious fairs, sports events which are locally called Melas. The community gatherings in the form of Melas are fantastic opportunities for the marketers. They can display the product, explain it or collect the prospect's data. Many times, the branding itself works very well. The stalls can be built in or around the Mela. The promoters should wear the branded T-shirts. A lot of activities for branding can be done like explaining the product through visual aids, interactive games, quiz competitions and even skits can be used for brand establishment. Free gifts like keychains, diaries, pens etc. can also be distributed for associating people with the brands. Automobile companies like cars and tractors use such activities. The tyre and farm mechanisation companies also do similar activities. The farmer fairs are organised by agriculture universities and agriculture departments at state and district levels. Farmers come here in large numbers for improving their knowledge and getting more information on the new technologies and products. Many agrochemical companies and other farming related companies participate in these fairs for better exposure.

Haat Bazaars:

In rural India there are weekly bazaars in a big ground normally called bazaars or Haat Bazaars. People go to buy groceries, daily needs, utensils, even motorcycles and cars in these Haat Bazaars. The agricultural implements and other agricultural support items are also available in these markets. Normally Haat Bazaars cover areas of 10 to 15 acres. The Haat Bazaars give a fantastic opportunity for marketers to showcase their products and services to the real customers on a first hand basis. Unlike fairs, these bazaars are weekly so the regular activity in these bazaars lead to quite interesting results, even leading to on the spot sales. A lot of activities like prospect data collection, explaining the product, nataks or other activities like local dances can be performed to associate the customers with the brand. The customer loyalty programs can also be initiated in such markets. Mostly FMCG companies campaign in these bazaars, but can be used by almost all the companies. The Prospects can be engaged digitally vis whatsapp bots or Facebook bots or via a platform for engagement.

Mandi Campaigns:

The grains produced in the farms come to the bazaars called Grain Markets or Mandis or Dana Mandis. These mandis contain all sorts of shops for the farmers so that they can buy agrochemicals, fertilisers and other items like groceries, mechanical items, etc. for their usage. So they regularly visit these mandis as and when required. Normally they visit more before sowing the new crops. These mandis are, therefore, a good opportunity for marketers to present their ideas to market their products.

Mandi campaigns can be of different types and different strategies can be used for these mandis. Some of them are dealer boards, gates and hoardings in mandis and connected villages branded with village boards. Another BTL activity used for the follow-up is the visual interaction and the hoardings, boards or the gates on the shops work as the follow-up brand activity. This activity is useful at the time of the sale or near major sale period.

This activity is very useful but the selection of the area where the hoarding or the board is to be put up or installed is very critical. In the case of hoarding, the position of the hoarding should be on a prominent road and should be visible when the customer is moving towards the city or market. If it is the other way round, it will be a sheer waste of money.

In the case of shop boards, gates and other shop branding items can be installed in the shops for highlighting the brand for visual follow-up.

The timing and position of these items is also very critical. To get the best ROI on this type of investment, it is best to install these inputs one month before the major sale period. Secondly, the placement of the inputs should be in such a way that it should be visible directly to the customer at his eye level. For instance, the installation of the shop board should be such that when the customer is approaching the shop or moving in the market, the board should come in his sight. The gate should be installed at the entrance and the banner should be placed behind the seat of the shopkeeper. In case of self-help stores, the banner should be at the place where the product is placed for the sale.

In this case, the selection of agency for efficient installation of the inputs is necessary. The selection of agency in the case of timely installation and right placement is required. So the marketers should select the agency very carefully.

Door to Door Campaigns:

In these campaigns, the promoters go to every house and explain the products and sell it on the spot. These campaigns help the customers to have first-hand experience of the products. The customer data is collected and sent to the call centre. The call centre cyclically intimates the customer for its purchase which helps in building a habit of using that product. The area is selected on the basis of the target audience.

This strategy can be used six months to a year to complete the cycle for the habit to be formed for using the product regularly. Such strategies help to build Brand Loyalty in the long run. These campaigns are done in Tier II, III and IV cities but not in villages. Mostly the FMCG companies go for these type of campaigns.

Influencer Campaigns:

The influencers are the people whose advice matters in their community. The influencers can be the Sarpanch of the village, the influential farmers, mechanics, carpenters, or any other skilled person in his craft.

Many companies do the influencer campaigns and they do it regularly. The concept behind the Influencer Meet is to educate the influencers about the product and appoint them as the brand's spokesperson. The influencers are identified on the basis of the industry; adhesive company like Fevicol uses carpenters, cement industry goes for mason meetings, agro input industry goes for the influential farmers, the tyre and tractor industry goes for mechanics, switches company like L&T goes for the electrician meets.

The L&T appoint electricians as their dealers as well.

The influencer meets are one of the most effective rural marketing strategy and it helps brands to build on long term basis.

Mass Campaigns:

Mass campaigns are basically an urban concept as in urban population there is a lot of homogeneity, whereas in rural areas there is a lot of diversity.

Mass campaigns use a lot of budget on mass media like TV, radio and print ads. The outdoor campaigns on big scale like hoardings, shop branding and vehicle campaigns are done on a big scale to influence the customer. The mass campaign is also very effective but only for the well established brands for next level brand positioning. In case of mass campaigns, the communication is very important as we cannot interact on one to one basis. Many FMCG companies like Coca Cola use such campaigns, even the government and political parties use them. This is very effective to build a brand within a short period of time on a large scale but the budgets required are very high.

These days there are TV campaigns possible on district wise using cable TV advertising and its penetration. Even statewide channels can be selected and the advertisement can be planned. The radio campaigns can be used for lead generation and concept based advertising is used for better ROI.

Digital Campaign:

Digital campaigns have already picked up the pace but with the lockdown in place for Covid-19, it has taken a forefront. Post corona, the importance of digitisation is going to be much more. Digital campaigns can be divided into multiple things like WhatsApp campaigns to the target audience and Facebook and Instagram ads, even the Tik Tok ads have taken a big leap now. So we need a social media strategy and proper content creation for all these media. The effectiveness of these advertisements depend upon the pre and post activities we do after these advertisements. We need to connect to the right customer, so we need proper research and clarity in mind as to who our customer is. Secondly, we have to know how to put the filters so that the advertisements hit the right ones. Wrong selection would lead to wastage of all the efforts. In the post advertisement phase, the linking of the advertisement should be with the proper landing page. The landing page is where the prospect reaches after clicking the advertisement. The content on the landing page should be such that the customer puts his details on it. Now a days, the interactive social media advertisements have also started. Interactive social media advertisements lure the prospect to play a game on the social media, like selecting a colour of his liking. Suppose he selects red, he will immediately get a message in his inbox from that company offering him a discount on a particular purchase, thereby luring him to buy. These AI applications can be used in WhatsApp and other media as well. We will discuss about it in detail in chapter 18 (Role of AI "Artificial Intelligence" in Rural Marketing).

360 Degree Campaign:

This is the most effective advertising and sales model which can be used in rural India. The purpose of 360 degree advertising model is to align all the activities and tools towards the ultimate goal of achieving sales along with brand building. This campaign is designed after taking the goals or sales target into account. First of all, the product analysis is done and the target audience is clearly described. Then we move towards the selection of the area of operation where this particular campaign is to be established. In this process, particular towns and villages are selected in order to work. Then we move towards the selection of the tools and activities which are to be used in advertising. We need to focus on the correct manpower selection for that purpose and it is very important that the manpower should be from those local areas only and should be well versed with them as well. Around the man power, a finance model is built which consists of all the activities which may include putting up posters, vehicle campaign, call centre, shop branding and many more. After the financial brick is formed, we need to build the structural network and start the reporting systems and measurement systems in order to measure the correct ROI of the campaign. We will discuss this model in detail in Chapter 14 (360 Degree Marketing and Sales Model).

Importance of Vernaculars:

In every activity, we should always collect the data and that data should be used to connect with the customer using call centres or using digital techniques like SMS or Voice mails. The call centres or messaging has to be in local language and dialect. If you need to connect to the Kashmiri apple growers, it has to be in Kashmiri. If you want the messaging to be in Hindi, then you need to have centres in Haryana, Lucknow, Patna or Ranchi so that the dialect matches it.

Using these strategies will provide the basis for a successful rural advertising campaign. That success, over multiple communities, can build the type of brand loyalty that creates real return on investment.

Why Rural Advertising Agency:

As we have already discussed, rural being very diverse, there is a need to understand rural very deeply. Understanding of the areas, dialect, culture, values and the traditions are very important in order to design and implement the campaign.

The mistake of misunderstanding can be very fatal. We had many such experiences during our work. Let me share one example with you.

We at Fateh Rural Pvt Ltd (www.fatehrural.com) were asked to print a particular leaflet of one of the agro input companies for Haryana, in Hindi of course. The leaflet design that came from Indore in Madhya Pradesh was also in Hindi. But when our rural team, who were handling Haryana, read the leaflet, they found that the Hindi was completely different than the kind used in Haryana. So, we translated the leaflet into the proper Hindi that the farmers in Haryana could understand. Here lies the importance of an experienced Agency.

Even the big urban advertising agencies don't have much reach and understanding of the rural India which leads to much higher expenses and lesser effectiveness in campaigns, hence leading to lesser sales.

CHAPTER 11

Focussing HNIs
of Rural India

Village elites are the progressive rural consumers, boasting high education and awareness levels. They desire the best in product quality, features and aesthetics. These elites are the high net worth farmers who hold large farm lands. They have high net worth in the form of assets and they sell large quantity of produce. Most entrepreneurs of rural India also come from these families but there are some who have built their fortunes by their hard work and struggle. There is another class of HNIs in Tier II and III cities. They are the executives of the corporates or government officials holding high positions. There are families as well where both the husband and wife are into jobs so these families have high incomes. The doctor families or the families whose children are studying in the high end private schools are another way of reaching the HNIs of Rural India. There is one more category of traders in all the small towns and mandis where these traders do all the business of sale and purchase. These families also make a lot of money and have good purchasing power. Focusing on these categories of people in Rural India will certainly help the marketers to reach deep down the pyramid.

The High Net-worth Farmers (HNF):

Every village have the high net worth farmers (HNF). HNFs hold 50% of the village land collectively. These farmers have large asset values and they use all the luxuries and are always in need of the latest products. The purchasing power of these people is much higher than even the average urban middle class. They use half of the total agri inputs used. They have major share of the tractor ownership and they are the families whose houses contain all the required lifestyle facilities.

Focusing on HNFs need a complete different strategy. Usually they don't even attend the farmer meetings where other marginal farmers come. They need special attention and respect for their presence to be heard. But they can be used as influencers in rural India as they are the successful ones in the village and almost everybody comes to them for the advice and everybody want to be close to them. The women in these families are also normally well educated and act as influencers or trend setters in the community. Connecting these families and creating their community would certainly help companies to influence them. Brands can use the special occasions to honour them for better reach in those villages.

The Entrepreneur of Rural India:

There are many entrepreneurs in rural India who have started their own professions like millers, small scale industrialists and the mechanical workshop owners, brick kiln owners, etc. These entrepreneurs make a good amount of money and have aspirations to live a good lifestyle. These entrepreneurs can be focused for brand positioning. They are also influencers as they are known in society and have relations with many people in the form of customers, vendors and employees. These families follow all the urban trends and expend on luxuries and expensive lifestyle utilities. The focus on these entrepreneur families could actually help. But connecting and influencing them is a real challenge. They can't be influenced the way HNFs can be influenced as they already have enough importance and honour in the society. But still they can be called on some business summits or on some family based gatherings for influence. Taking an example, an automobile brand can have an industry specific summit and call the entrepreneurs to showcase the brand during the summit. During the visit they can have a look and feel about the product. These tips may be useful to the marketers.

Senior Executives in Corporates:

Another class is of the executives in corporates like zonal heads, regional heads, etc. This class is the most difficult to influence. But it's very easy to explain the advantages of brands to them, as they understand it very well. They are brand conscious people, therefore, selling them the brands becomes a challenge. They are well educated, aware and well-travelled people who are well versed with the utilities and the value of the brands. They understand the value of the brand in the form of utility and standard of living. In many of these families, their spouses are also in jobs so the family income is high. They understand the value of education, health and awareness. They invest a lot in the education of their children and also put a lot of money on their health. These families understand nutrition and the value of food so invest a lot on healthy food and good brands available in the market. These families can be focussed via digital and mass media campaigns. One to one could be quite challenging for them as they have less time for such activities. The 360 Degree digital model can be really useful for such people.

Salaried Couple Families:

The rise in women education have led to women doing jobs in government offices, corporates, banks, insurance companies, schools and colleges. These women with jobs create the salaried couples, where both the spouses work and have fixed salaries every month. These families save at least one salary for future and they can use one salary to run the family. These families have larger scope to purchase better things for their children and for themselves. As they have a better family income so the banks and other financial institutions also support them with finance which they take for buying their homes or buying cars in the form of home loans and car loans. Some even use personal loans to buy other lifestyle and utility things. These families' major expense is on education but they live a decent lifestyle as well. These families can be focused and influenced using digital media, mass media or with personal touch. They are quite influenced with mass media but still they are connected with roots. So there is good impact of culture on them. The cultural fairs and the local market branding could impact them well. Even the peer influencers do work with them well. The retailers can also influence them.

Government Officials:

There is a class of government officials in rural India. They have secure jobs and get salaries always on time and many even get pensions. They are the people working in schools, electricity departments, PSUs, corporations, mandi boards, etc. This class is connected with the culture as well, but enjoy a lifestyle. They have good purchasing power and are influenced by the peer group or by the seniors. They can be influenced via mass media like TV, newspapers and now even with social media like WhatsApp and Facebook. They can also be invited to the functions in some hotels for the product displays. Normally they always go for the marketing fairs so can be influenced there as well. The one to one or door to door campaigns can also work very well on them.

CBSE and ICSE Schools in Rural India:

Rural India understands the meaning of the education and want their children to study in best of the schools. Because of this demand of best education in rural India, we could see a lot of private schools opened across the country. The best schools are affiliated to the CBSE or ICSE boards. The top layer of rural India believes in admitting their children in these schools only. These schools have become a place for marketing different products. Taking an example, stationery companies like Camlin regularly do the painting competitions on national basis in these schools. Colgate promotes its product during the healthy teeth campaign which focusses on the habit of brushing teeth twice on a daily basis. Similar activities happen in these schools connected with the brands. The innovations could help make the children your brand ambassadors. The TV media and one to one campaigns in schools could influence them very well. Many brands can be associated with better education and habit and character building of the children. The brands can even sponsor the annual programs of the schools where the children as well as their parents participate. They can get the chance to interact with the customers as well.

Professionals:

There are professionals in all Tier III and IV towns like lawyers, CAs, doctors, etc. Some families are into the same profession. Most professionals are rich and they make a good amount of money. They are living a good life style and follow the community standards. The purchasing capacity of these professionals and their families is quite good. We could focus on these professionals by sponsoring their events like Lawyer Association meetings or CA Institutes Annual Conference, etc. Brands could connect with them through their professions or through their hobbies. These people have less time to waste so if the brand is connected to their profession, it could work like "coffee for professionals."

Traders of Rural India:

The role of traders in Rural India's growth is tremendous. The distributor network of every brand and company, big and small, Indian or multinational, food, medicines, cement, anything which is sold, goes through these traders. The traders are the bricks of the economic structure of this country. They invest money and sell the products to the end customers. This class is the richest class of all and have enough purchasing power. They invest in every way, in property, in stocks and in products. They change professions with time and travel to distant places for business. This class is the class where the brands should focus mostly. The influence of TV and newspaper as well as the interest of using luxury items to show off the wealth is also a part of this class's culture. Building the brands in this community would make brands much bigger as they are the biggest influencers in the market. The companies use different ways to build these influencers. Different schemes and packages are offered to connect and build distributors.

The HNIs of rural India are the most important part of the commercial activity. Although they are only 30% of the total population but own 70% of the resources of the country. They act as influencers as well. Focusing on these people will certainly help brands to reach the masses.

CHAPTER 12

Digital Marketing and Rural Call Centres

The word 'digital' has become the buzzword these days. I call it virtual Interaction. Virtual interaction seems much easier but it is not the case. Had it been so, many companies would have been selling just through apps and would have been profitable. The real thing is that virtual connection with the customer is not that easy and a lot of effort is required to keep the customer engaged for a long time. There are a number of solutions in the virtual interaction services like call centres, apps, SMS, voice calls and even the portals. But in spite of all these solutions, the company has to build a complete first hand, one to one interaction at the customer level and the interaction may be in the form of the marketing guy, field development people, a delivery boy or the retailer or distributor support executive. There are a number of ways to do the virtual interaction with the customer like call centres in local languages with local dialect, SMS, voice calls, etc.

Why Rural Call Centres:

One of the oldest way of connecting with the customer is the cold call or the follow-up call. Nowadays such service is supported by servers and software to measure and get maximum efficiency from the executives and is called a call centre service.

In the case of the rural market, the call centre is one of the important activity but it is still used in an amateur way. India is a diverse country having multiple languages and dialects, so we need to interact with customers in local languages or dialects which is not possible from a single location. Some companies have tried to do it from a single location which has led to lack of clarity in the communication with the deepest part of the country. For that, the marketers have to build a network of call centres at multiple locations for the solutions and other follow-up services in their native languages. Or the companies can hire services from companies like Fateh Rural which are into multi locational call centre services in vernaculars. Multiple services through call centres can be used like the customer care handling which can lead to immediate solution to the customer, leading to customer satisfaction on the spot, which may lead to brand loyalty.

The call centres can also be used to market or advertise in the form of information service to customer about a new product, or a survey or a market fad can be understood through the vibes from the customer. Some companies use the call centres for the first level lead generation which could lead to better conversion rate.

The efficacy of the call centre depends on the database. Better the database, better will be the result and the ROI. So the data-base generation can be done by collecting data during the campaigns which have been mentioned earlier like vehicle campaigns or one to one contact marketing and digital marketing. This type of data collection will lead to better quality data collection and will generate more number of convertible leads.

We can use the SMS and voice call services also. These services are used like the mass media where in a single go, millions of messages can be broadcasted in a single day. It is a good method for follow-up or information broadcasting. Even mediums like WhatsApp can also be used although each service has its constraints.

Running a Rural Call Centre:

Rural call centre services are always in need, almost every company is using these services. Some are having some in-house callers sitting at their regional offices with just a mobile phone and a list of customer data on excel sheet. Some have proper call centres set up at a single location. But both ways are having constraints. In the first one, no recording or voice training is done and is run in a completely unprofessional manner with manual calling. The inefficiency certainly hits such call centre setups. In the second one, the infrastructure costs goes too high and the focus is also diluted. In a central call centre facility, matching the dialects and rural language becomes a major challenge as mostly the facilities are in metros. The companies do not get the executives who have rural background or rural connect. Also, India being an extremely diverse country with thousands of dialects, the heart to heart connection with the rural customer becomes a major challenge as the dialect do not match.

So the solution is to outsource the call centres to the rural agencies who have multi locational setups in deep rural India. Firstly, the call centre executives working in these agencies have deeper roots and connections with rural India. If a call centre is for Kashmir, it should be somewhere in Kashmir like 60–70 km inside Srinagar, so that the dialect should match. This way we are able to create jobs in deep rural areas as well. Secondly, with a professional rural call centre agency all types of trainings like voice training, marketing pitch and product trainings are regularly imparted to the executives for better efficacy. The reporting is also done in a structured format which will be useful in analysing and leads conversion. The data analytics services can also be taken for better understanding of the actions we have taken and for the future course of action.

Rural call centres can be used in multiple ways. I would like to talk about a few innovative ways.

Handling Customer Care Through Toll-Free Services:

Many companies use toll-free services for a direct connection with their customers. Normally toll-free service uses IVR. IVR is where the dealer is redirected to the server, which connects him with the options that he has to choose by dialling 1, 2, 3 or 9 and then finally he is connected to the call centre executive, if required. This is where the real challenge comes for the rural companies. India has 16 major languages. If a customer has to choose his language, he have to wait till 16 options are given to him. It is pretty obvious that under such circumstances, the customer will never return to such a toll-free service. This is where the solutions are needed on technology basis where the toll-free is programmed in such a way that if a rural customer calls, his call should be automatically routed to the executive of his respective language. If a caller is calling from Guntur in Andhra Pradesh, his call should be redirected automatically to the Telugu executive. The first word he should listen to should be Telugu. That is when he will feel at home and will be open to talk about his problems or requirements. We will be able to establish a rapport with him.

The second challenge which comes while running a customer care number is where to put this facility. Normally such facilities are put in metros. But putting them in metros make them very expensive. Secondly we don't get callers for all languages of India from one city. Even if we somehow get people of all languages, the real challenge comes when their dialect doesn't match with the rural dialect of the same language. The urban callers are not able to establish a rapport with the rural customers leading to a wasted effort. So the customer care facility for any rural company needs a multiple setup, that too, in deep rural pockets where the languages as well as the dialect matches. The call centre executives from small cities have deep connection with rural and they build the rapport with the rural customer very easily.

The third challenge is the training of the executives. Two types of trainings are required for the efficient running of the calls. They are product training and the marketing pitch. Both the trainings are required in the local language. The effectiveness of the toll-free completely depend on the training of the executives. Better the training, better is the satisfaction and better the customer loyalty. If the call centre is in the same state near the regional office of the company, the regional team can visit the centre regularly for the product training and even watch the progress. The marketing pitch is made by the agency, so you need an agency who has experience in rural marketing. The marketing pitch can do wonders if built properly in the local language.

The reports should be generated on a daily basis with the hot leads either converted or transferred to the sales staff. Data analytics can be done and future actions can be planned accordingly.

The call centre executives should be given answers to the FAQs. If a particular question is not covered in the FAQs, then it should be escalated to the concerned personnel from the company who is stipulated for the job.

The toll-free number can be advertised on all other advertising media like vehicle campaigns, cable TV Ads, POP materials etc. The use of toll-free can make your customer connected with you for a longer period of time. You can cross sell or up-sell through the toll-free as well. You can also run loyalty programs through toll-free. Many problems in the market become visible and by taking action, brand position can be improved.

Out Bound Marketing Calls:

Marketing calls made to the potential customers can be done from call centres. These outbound calls can be either for product introduction or corporate branding or product promotion. These calls are made in local languages. WhatsApp or SMS campaigns are used for follow-up. These calls are used for cross selling and up-selling. The pitch can be changed during the season, pre-season or post-season calls. The outbound call centre is also used for lead generation. The hot leads are forwarded to the local sales team. The influencers like dealers, retailers, Sarpanches and other influential farmers are also called for any improvement in brand recognition. The reporting is done on daily basis. Later the data analytics can also be done.

Such call centres are very useful for the 360 degree marketing and sales model. Here, the call centres role is to identify the focussed customer from the data collected via various sources like field force, vehicle campaign, POP material, toll-free or missed call service. The identification of the focussed customer is done on the basis of parameters defined by the company. This data is shared with sales leading to a better follow-up. These focussed customers are influenced through WhatsApp, voice call and SMS campaigns. These activities improve the chances of conversion and motivate the field staff. Using the outbound services with effective manner can improve the sales by a good percentage.

Surveys Through Call Centre:

Surveys have always helped businesses to analyse and grow. The surveys are done on a one to one basis with a questionnaire. The disadvantage of actually going to a place and getting a survey done is that it takes a lot of effort and costs a lot of money. Nowadays, a lot of tele surveys are done for different objectives. These call centres can also be used for the surveys. The data can be analysed further to decide on a future course of action. Surveys like completion presence, brand positioning, price band determination, etc. can be done with the help of call centres.

Payment Collection Services:

Payment collection from the customers has always been a pain for almost all companies. Payment collection can be done with the help of the call centres. The call centre executives are fed with the data from the ERP like SAP regularly. This is the data for overdue payments. The callers call the distributors for payment and the collection information is uploaded on the system. The callers also inform the sales staff as and when required. This system improves the payment collection. Sometimes the distributors block the call centre numbers, so the numbers are changed on a rotation basis for the calls to go through server based calling. This service reduces the time used by sales staff on payment collection and helps them to focus more on sales.

Order Collection Services:

The order collection activity can be run successfully from the call centres. The list of the distributors with zero or low pending payments are taken from the ERP and the orders are collected from such distributors. The distributors can call and place the orders as well. Order collection improves the number of orders as the number of customers connected per day improves and this builds the ordering process as well.

Digital Marketing Services and Apps:

The digital media or the internet media which is the buzzword these days have made many billionaires. Every company is trying to use this internet wave and earn a fortune for themselves. No need to mention that every single day a large number of Indians are riding the internet so it seems that it is easy to connect with them which actually may not be the case. Even in the internet space, there is a lot of clutter. There are millions of sites and thousands of apps trying to be on the small space of a smart phone. So how to make an app which is visible and which will reach the maximum number of users? The big question of reaching out and a perpetual connection to the real customer is hitting everybody's mind. I believe the best customer service will be the king.

In digital marketing, the number of activities can be identified and done. The social media groups and social media interaction with customers and the paid campaigns on social media can be done. The major social media sites like Facebook, LinkedIn, Instagram and many others are used for direct interaction with clients. Even the SEO and marketing on major search engines like Google and Yahoo would also help to reach the customer with ease.

360 degree Digital Lead Generation Model:

The most important thing about digital is not likes or shares rather its lead generation. The utilisation of digital technologies is to build a platform for better engagement of the customers for longer periods for better brand recall and improving sales. In this model alignment and integration all digital channels like Facebook, Whatsapp, Youtube, Google, Linkedin and others is done via an external platform.

The second point is automatic interaction with the customers using Artificial Intelligence and Bots. Due to regular interaction the leads are captured and send to the call centre or the field force for further filtration. These leads are connected via field force and are converted. Many other technologies are used for the long term engagements like RSS feeds, Links sharing and Governmental scheme sharing with the customers for better rapport and caring. Even the webinars and the videos are shared and recorded at the platform for future reference. This video library can act like Farmer TV for the farmers, or other rural customers.

Major objectives of the 360 degree Digital Lead Generation Model is to improve the digital foot print of the company. It also helps in improving the engagement with the customers using different tools and social media platforms. The model helps in improving the lead generation through all channels and helps with better engagement with the existing data which company have collected earlier. This model also helps in integrating the trade network for better digital presence, brand visibility and sales. The integration with the Media and outdoor activities with the digital model would improve the effectiveness of campaigns by multifold. This model helps in improving sales and also improves in cross-selling and up-selling.

We will be discussing more about digital technologies in the upcoming chapter on Artificial Intelligence and Automation.

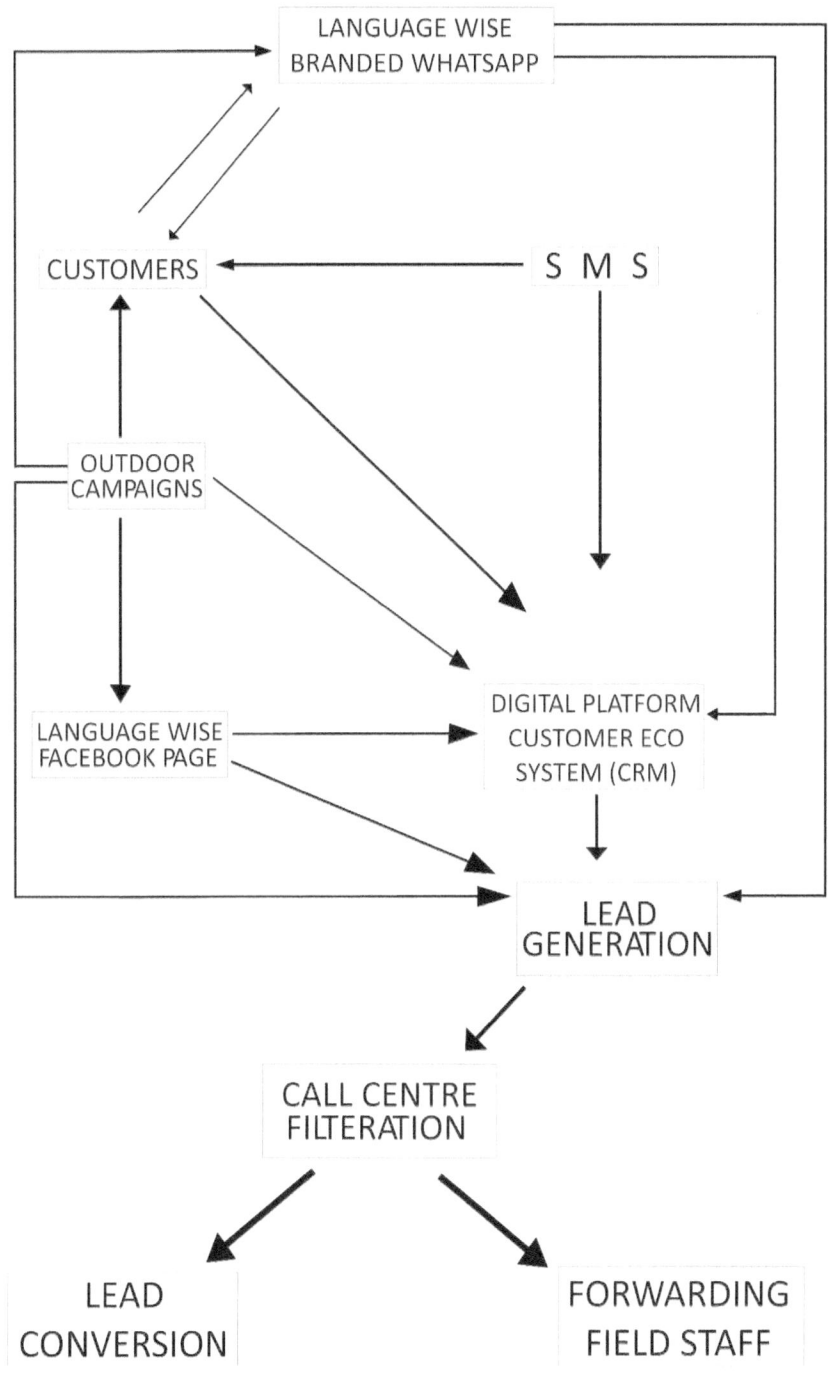

TYPE TO ENTER A CAPTION.

CHAPTER 13

Conventional and Unconventional Rural Advertising

There are multiple ways to connect with the customer in rural India. Some of the methods are conventional and are a part of every rural campaign like vehicle campaigns, hoardings, wall paintings, etc. But there are some which are new innovations to reach the rural customer with a difference. Working with the brands since many years I have been through many methods of advertising and marketing, mostly used to mention here.

Conventional Methods:

Conventional methods which have been in use since many years have been discussed here. These methods which are considered conventional in rural India are actually much different and new in comparison to the methods used in urban India. These methods are a must for marketing and advertising the brands in rural India. Almost all companies use it and almost all marketers have to go through these methods. Some of the most common ones are discussed here.

Mass Media and Design Services:

Communication design should be in local language taking into account local culture as well. The design and the translation should be done by the proper agency which knows about rural India and connects with the respective regions through nativity. The colours and the message should be very simple and clear for the people to understand. The communication should connect the brand with the people. Video content should be in the regional language and should be in the local dialect and the culture shown should also be local. The dubbed advertisements, normally used by many FMCG advertisers, lose their effectiveness and connection. An advertisement showing a Punjabi guy dubbed in Bhojpuri won't connect with the audience. Telecast of the videos should be done on the regional and cable channels. There are many local newspapers and magazines like Agro One in Marathi and Kheti Duniya in Punjabi and Hindi prevalent in Punjab and Haryana should also be used for the better reach of the brands.

The selection of the channels and media buying strategy is of utmost importance while choosing the different mass media channels. In the case of TV channels telecasting and radio broadcasting, the selection of the channels and the allocation of budget to every channel is a critical step. Experienced Rural Agencies are required for such planning.

Outdoor Services:

Outdoor services connect with the people on one to one basis and influences them in much better way. Outdoor advertising can be done in multiple ways and we can use multiple means to reach the rural consumer. Different services are used for different impact and stage of the product. Some services are used for the introduction of the brand and some are used for brand follow up and reminder. Others are used for mass connection of the brand. The outdoor services which are commonly used for Brand awareness are mentioned below.

Vehicle Campaign:

Be it a political campaign for PM candidate or the campaign for Swachh Bharat or the LED bulb distribution to the Reliance Jewellers showrooms in Tier III cities or the Biotechnology Brand Bollgard by Monsanto, all need vehicle campaign to reach the rural India. In the case of campaigns we can use the vehicles with different ways like Led campaigns, promoter based campaigns, nukkad natak/magician/dance group campaigns, customised games for concept promotion. The vehicle campaign is one of the most used BTL activity for one to one interaction with the customer. We can use this activity for demand generation, introduction of product and first-hand experience of the customer with the product. We can also feel the pulse of the market by this activity.

Hoardings in Grain Markets, Mandis, Village Boards, Dealer Boards and Gates:

Another BTL activity used for the follow-up is the visual display. The hoardings, boards or the gates on the shops work as the follow-up brand activity. This activity is useful at the time of the sale or near major sale period. This activity is very useful but the selection of the area where the hoarding or the board is to put or installed is very critical. In the case of hoarding, the position of the hoarding should be on the prominent road and should be on the side facing the direction in which the customer is moving towards the city or market. If it is other way round, it will be a sheer waste of money. In the case of shop; boards, gates and other shop branding items can be installed in the shops for highlighting the brand for visual follow-up. The timing and position of these items is also very critical. To get the best ROI on this type of investment, it is best to install these inputs one month before the major sale period. Secondly, the placement of the inputs should be in such a way that it should be visible directly to the customer at his eye level. For instance, the installation of the shop board should be such that when the customer is approaching the shop or moving in the market the board should come in his sight. At the entrance the gate should be installed, the banner should be placed behind the seat of the shopkeeper. In case of self-help stores, the banner should be at the place where the product is placed for the sale. In this case, the selection of the agency for efficient installation of the inputs is necessary. The selection of agency in the case of timely installation and right placement is required. So the marketers should select the agency very carefully.

Wall Painting, Digital Wall Painting, Shop Painting:

Wall paintings are an effective and economical medium for advertising in rural areas. They are silent unlike traditional theatre. A speech or film comes to an end, but wall painting stays as long as the weather allows it to. Retailer normally welcomes paintings of their shops, walls and name boards since it makes the shop look cleaner and better. Their shops look alluring and stand out among other outlets. Besides, rural households shopkeepers and panchayats do not accept any payment for their wall to be painted with product messages. To get one's wall painted with the product messages is looked upon as a status symbol. The greatest advantage of the medium is the power of the picture, complete with its local touch. The images used have a strong emotional association with the surrounding, a feat impossible for even a moving visual medium like television, which must use general image to cater to the greatest number of viewers. Digital wall painting is the printed material directly pasted on the wall. Very complex computer designs can also be printed and pasted on the wall and the brand can be displayed in a better way.

Gift Items:

Gift items required for free distribution during campaigns are keychains with prototype of the product, caps, t-shirts, purses, mobile covers, hand fans, etc. When the one to one activity is done, the gift items have a big role in branding and positioning of the product as the gift items remain with them after the meeting for long and the brand printed on it hits the consumer's mind for long and helps to retain or acquire the customer.

POP Materials:

In every meeting with the customer we need to give some POP or printed material for brand awareness. The types of materials are leaflets, brochures, etc. The brochure or leaflet design is the key to making an impact on the customers. The pictorial and detailed USPs and the explanation of the usefulness of the product or service will work. The gift items vary with the area of operation and regional preferences. The gamcha works well in Eastern India. The gift items also change with the situation as with the rise in corona cases in India there is a demand for sanitizers, masks, gloves and other such items for free distribution. Through this, companies do some work for societies and build their brand as responsible corporates in the communities.

Kissan Melas, Haat Bazaars and Exhibitions:

India is a country of religious melas and cultural events where people gather and many economic activities happen. Many agricultural universities and departments also go for farmer fairs or agri events for the introduction of best practices in agriculture and introduction of new technologies in agriculture. Brand participation in these fairs certainly helps to give access to the target audience. The effectiveness of the events will depend on the amount of customer interaction and the type of interaction. Brand awareness will certainly depend on various factors like what type of event or activity is being performed during the customer interaction and whether the concerned activity is attracting the right customer or not. The activity may include direct exposure to the product, showcasing the demonstration at the event, explanation of the product using AV medium or using a nukkad natak team. Various methodologies are used to develop a relationship with the customer. Such events can be used to collect the database or generate leads for the product or service. Many methodologies are used for collection of database like collecting mobile numbers for the lucky draw which can be done at the stipulated time or in just 15 minutes after the coupons are filled. In those 15 to 30 minutes, the team can explain the brand to the customer and at the lucky draw the brand showcase can be done in a big way.

Bus Panelling and Local Auto Rickshaw Branding:

Buses and rickshaws as well as the local share taxis are used for transportation in rural India. These modes of transportation can also be used for brand awareness. Buses, the share taxis and rickshaws can decorated with panels printed with brand communications on them. As they move from village to village, they act as moving billboards. Even the auto rickshaw drivers can be made brand ambassadors for the brands as they can send leads through app while doing their job and earn some extra income. We at Fateh Rural have done some experiments for brand promotion in the buses in Punjab through video

CDs as many buses use videos, films or songs in their buses through an Led TV fitted in them. We gave video CDs with popular songs and advertisements pre-loaded in them which many bus drivers used and the brand was promoted.

Bus Stand and Mandi Branding:

Bus stand and the mandis are the most active places in rural India where people travel to and buy things for their needs. These two places can be branded with bill boards, hoardings and other POP materials like posters, 3D posters etc. Many more activities like nukkad nataks or the introduction of brands or lead generation can be done in these areas while interacting with customers. These places can be major places for branding and effective marketing. There are many small vendors in this area doing some jobs like tea stall etc. who can also be used for lead generation and even selling of the brand.

Unconventional Methods:

We have discussed about the conventional means of advertising in rural India. But with the rise in infrastructure and facilities in the rural space, there are many opportunities for marketers for branding their products. They can use different media for such activities, some of them are discussed below.

All India Rural ATM's Branding:

The use of ATMs is increasing day by day. The penetration of the ATMs in rural India is significant. Not only banks but many third party agencies are also installing ATMs and they are maintaining it themselves. These agencies and banks offer many branding opportunities for the companies as normally ATM is used by the responsible and decision makers in the family. The offerings by the ATMs include a board over the ATM cabin, a sandy inside, a branded screen and the branding on the balance confirmation slips. These branding solutions can influence the customers in rural areas.

Measurement of Cable TV Advertisements:

Cable TV being localised in nature, is deeply connected with the regional people. With the digitalisation of cable networks, there is a huge change in the cable TV organisation. Today almost all cable TV channels are connected digitally at a central server. The advertising can be monitored, controlled and designed at the central level for all the channels in India. With this technology we can now plan the cable TV advertisements just like the main stream TV media. The advertisements budgets can be allocated as per the brand requirement of hitting the target consumers. The cable TV also offers the strips or special programmes like local news or latest on-demand movies. These peculiarities improves their TRP in the rural areas. Even the dashboard is provided for the live telecasting report. The marketers can make this media a part of their branding strategy as well.

Local Transportation Branding:

Logistic companies use trucks and trailers for the transportation of goods across the country. These companies have started offering branding solutions on all sides of the trucks for rural India. It is similar to bus branding. The local transports of Tata Ace and other such utility vehicles can also be used for the branding purposes.

Building Local Brand Ambassadors:

Companies use celebrities for their brand promotion. But India being a diverse society, the national stars do not cater to every part and are very expensive as well. Every region has its own stars and celebrities in the form of singers, comedians and regional film actors. People connect themselves with these actors easily as they speak the regional language and represent the local culture. The Punjabi singers, Bhojpuri actors, South Indian stars and Marathi TV stars are some of the prominent examples. The stars can be used for the endorsement on TV and mass advertising. They can be used for particular events for mass gatherings. They can also be used for new stores openings or product launchings. The cost of these stars is much lesser than the national stars and the celebrities can be chosen for specific regions wherever required as per the brand position and presence. These strategies could give better results.

Involving Self Help Groups:

Self-help groups are the groups made up mostly of women in rural areas who work together and sell something made locally by them. These women groups are supported by the government and the local and national NGOs. The marketers can use these groups for propagation of the branding activities by associating the brand with these groups. Health initiatives can be started by the nutrient and Ayurveda companies, cleanliness by the soap and sanitiser companies and the concept of self-reliance and confidence by the sports and yoga based companies. Education initiatives can be started by the stationery and geometry box manufacturers. There can be many aspects and many more innovations to involve the self-help groups for brand awareness as well as improving their lives.

Village Adoption by Brands:

Villages need a lot of care and village adoption is one of the ways to do it. Corporates being socially responsible, can give back to the society in this way. The villages can be supported in multiple ways in the form of educational support and development. Career counselling, guidance and support can help youngsters. The entrepreneurship development can be an important activity. Helping in getting drinking water, agricultural awareness about new technologies, financial options and government schemes can be few of them. The brand association with these activities can build a strong relationship with these people and they can serve as the brand ambassadors for the Company.

Cultural and Religious Fairs Participation:

Other than agricultural fairs, participation in the religious and cultural fairs can be a very good step for brand awareness. The presence of the brand in local fairs connects the brand with the local populace. The communication required here is completely local and should connect with the people. The brand awareness created here can have long term effects. The activities can be broadcasted through live video broadcast, through media and through video messages to the consumers for the far reaching effects of the activity. The community can be built around such fairs by connecting through digital media.

There are multiple ways to connect with the customers in rural India. I have discussed a few of them but there are many more which will be invented and designed with innovation for better connections.

CHAPTER 14

360 Degree Marketing and Sales Model

360 Degree Marketing and Sales Model align all the activities, agencies and vendors towards the achievement of the company's goal. This model helps to maximise the ROI (Return on Investment). The ROI is measured in real terms and is monitored on real time basis. The actions are taken accordingly in order to get desired results.

Every marketing activity starts with a goal. To achieve that goal, different activities are planned, different agencies and vendors are hired. All the agencies and the vendors are controlled by the marketing managers of the companies. Sometimes, the activities are aligned but the vendors and agencies are not aligned. Secondly, the marketing plans do not monitor sales on real time basis. The measurement of ROI is also done on factors other than sales. The misalignment of marketing and sales leads to erratic results.

In order to solve this problem, the 360 Degree Marketing and Sales Model came into existence. In this model, all the activities are optimally planned. Secondly, alignment and monitoring of all the activities are done on real time basis. All the parameters point towards the product sales.

First of all, a product analysis and a market survey is done in order to understand the brand positioning and market potential of the product in a particular area. The target audience is identified and sale targets are set. After selecting the towns and the respective villages, advertising activities and tools are selected and planned.

Experienced field manpower is recruited as required. A financial brick is developed around which the whole building of marketing campaign is built. The model starts with the data collection supported by a call centre and branding activities. The leads are generated and converted through field force and followed up through call centre. The branding is done at retailer level, in the selected villages and towns. Electronic media and print media is used for the mass campaigns and digital media is used for specific hitting. Sales are monitored and actions are taken as per requirement. Reports are generated on daily basis and sales are ensured. After the completion of the campaign, the feedback is taken and planning for the next phase is done. The 360 Degree Model can work wonders, it is explained as follows.

Product and Market Analysis:

Market survey is done by interacting with dealers, distributors and retailers. The customers are interviewed for more clarity on the product clarity and brand positioning. On the basis of the earlier sales report and confidence of the distributors, specific dealers or retailers are selected. This retailer selection helps in selection of area for operation. With the help of the retailer's geographical area, the target audience is selected. This is how we get the number of retailer shops to be covered in a particular area. This number will help us in multiple ways to calculate the branding cost and sale conversion ratio.

Sales Target and Target Audience:

360 Degree Model analyses the sales target and then plans the areas to be covered. After the retailers are finalised, a survey is done with the retailers about the area which is connected with that particular retailer. The target audience is finalised and branding is planned for the selected areas, with may include towns, some villages and market places. The target prospect is defined and identified correctly. The number of prospect touch points are finalised and the campaign is started with a specific sales conversion ratio. The sale conversion ratio is finalised on the basis of the analytics of the previous experiences and other factors.

Selection of Towns and Villages:

The list of towns and villages is taken from the retailers. The particular town or village area which come to a specific retailer is identified with the help of the retailers. Village population, distance from the nearest town, brand positioning are some of the factors behind the selection.

Advertisement Tools Selection:

Many advertisement tools can be used for the 360 degree model. The campaign starts with designing services. Communication design should be in the local language, taking into account the local culture as well. The design and the translation should be done by the proper agency which knows about rural India and connects with the respective regions through nativity. The colours and the messages should be very simple and clear for the people to understand. The communication should connect the brand with the people.

For mass media campaigns, we need videos to be designed. Video content should be in the regional language and should be in the local dialect. The culture shown should also be local. The dubbed advertisements, as normally used by many FMCG advertisers, lose their effectiveness and connection. An advertisement showing a Punjabi guy but dubbed in Bhojpuri will not connect with the audience. Telecast of the videos should be done on the regional and cable channels. There are many local newspapers and magazines like Agro One in Marathi and Kheti Duniya in Punjabi and Hindi prevalent in Punjab and Haryana that should also be used for the better reach of the brands.

The outdoor campaigns are required for village to village interaction with the customers. The best way to connect with customers is vehicle campaigns. Be it a political campaign for the PM candidate or the campaign for Swachh Bharat or the LED bulb distribution to the Reliance Jewellers showrooms in tier III cities or the Biotechnology Brand Bollgard by Monsanto, all need vehicle campaign to reach the rural India. In the case of campaigns, we can use the vehicles with different ways like Led campaigns, promoter based campaigns, Nukkad natak/magician/dance group campaigns and customised games for concept promotion. The vehicle campaign is one of the most used BTL activity for the one to one interaction with the customer. We can use this activity for demand generation, introduction of product and first-hand experience of the customer with the product. We can also feel the pulse of the market by this activity. During these activities, data is collected and sent to the call centres for follow-ups.

The field force uses POP material and gift items during the campaigns in villages and towns. In every meeting with the customer, we need to give some POP or printed material for the brand awareness. The types of materials are leaflets, brochures, etc. The brochure or leaflet design is the key to making an impact on the customers. The pictorial and detailed USPs and the explanation of the usefulness of the product or service will work. Gift Items are required for free distribution during campaigns like keychains with prototype of the product, caps T-shirts, purses, mobile covers, hand fans, etc. When the one to one activity is done, the gift items have a big role in branding and positioning of the product as the gift items remain with them after the meeting for long and the brand printed on it hits the consumer's mind for long and helps to retain or acquire the customer.

The events and participation in Kissan Melas, Haat Bazaars and Exhibitions also help to build the brand. India is a country of the religious melas and cultural events where people gather and many economic activities happen. Many agricultural universities and departments also go for farmer fairs or agri events for the introduction of best practices in agriculture and introduction of new technologies in agriculture. The brand participation in these fairs certainly helps to give access to the target audience. The effectiveness of the events will depend on the amount of customer interaction and the type of interaction. The brand awareness will certainly depend on various factors like what type of event or activity is being performed during the customer interaction.

Manpower Selection:

Experienced manpower is selected for the branding and sales activities. Candidates who are well versed with local areas are taken for the job. After selection, two types of trainings are done. One is the technical training about the product and some FAQs about the product. The purpose of this training is to give field staff complete information about the product and the company. The second training is about branding and sales. In this training, proper use of the POP material is taught. In order to utilise every leaflet properly, field staff is trained. The sales training consists of the sales pitch and the presentation. Field staff is trained about the handling of the meeting and closing of the sales. These trainings are very crucial for the effectiveness of the campaigns.

Building a Finance Model Brick:

A model is built around the field executive where he is associated with retailers on one side and prospects and customers on the other. The number of contact points are calculated and contacted through the field executives. All the costs associated in this exercise like that of call centre, POP materials, branding and other expenses are included in the cost of the field executives using the Brick model.

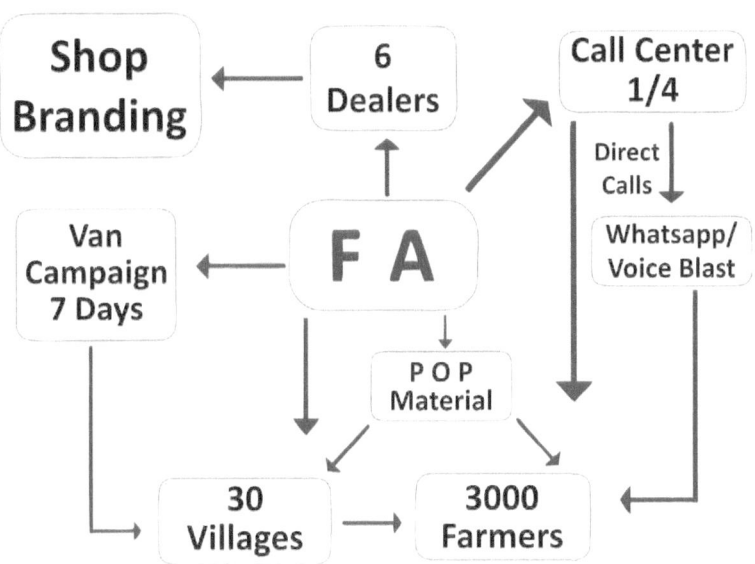

Building Structural Network of Advertising and Sales Model:

On the basis of the Brick model and considering the sales target, complete network and structure of 360 degree model is built. In this model, the field executive meets the customers, collects data and gives presentation about the product. The branding in villages and markets are done for brand visibility. The branding includes putting up posters, boards, hoardings, wall paintings, shop branding, vehicle campaigns, etc. The data collected is transferred technologically to the call centres. The call centre analyses the data and categorises into a, b and c categories, taking into account the different parameters. Then the follow-up and digital campaigns like WhatsApp, SMS, or voice calls are done to influence the customer.

Branding:

Village, shop branding and market branding are the major branding activities done in this campaign.

The hoardings, boards or the gates on the shops work as the follow-up brand activity. This activity is useful at the time of the sale or near major sale period. This activity is very useful but the selection of the area where the hoarding or the board is to be put up or installed is very critical. In the case of hoarding, the position of the hoarding should be on the prominent road and should be on the side visible to the customer when the customer is moving towards the city or market. If it is the other way round, it will be a sheer waste of money. In the case of shop boards, gates and other shop branding items can be installed in the shops for highlighting the brand for visual follow-up. The timing and position of these items is also very critical. To get the best ROI on this type of investment is to install these inputs one month before the major sale period. Secondly, the placement of the inputs should be in such a way that it should be visible directly to the customer at his eye level. For instance, the installation of the shop board should be such that when the customer is approaching the shop or moving in the market the board should come in his sight. At the entrance, the gate should be installed and the banner should be placed behind the seat of the shopkeeper. In case of self-help stores, the banner should be where the product is placed for the sale. And in this case the selection of agency for efficient installation of the inputs is necessary. The selection of agency in the case of timely installation and right placement is required. So the marketers should select the Agency very carefully. Branding can be done at important public places. Bus stands and the Mandis are the most active places in rural India where people travel and buy things for their needs. These two places can be branded with bill boards, hoardings and other POP materials like posters, 3D posters etc. Shop branding can be done at the time of sale.

Implementation and Reporting:

An account manager is appointed for the complete implementation, control and reporting of the project. Reports are generated on daily, weekly and monthly basis. Call centre generates the reports on daily basis. The major reports consist of the number of customers contacted by the field staff, daily lead generation, daily sales monitoring and daily follow-up calls by the call centre staff. The weekly and monthly report goes to the state head and is about the analytics and sales leads and conversion. Reporting format is shared at the starting of the projects. The data is analysed and reports are directed to take action.

Sales Conversion Monitoring:

During the sales period, monitoring is done carefully by tracking the retailers on a daily basis. The call centre and the field staff coordinate with each other for generation and conversion of the sales leads. The major purpose of monitoring the sales conversion during the season is to take action in the area where the sales are not moving as per expectation. Pushing sales in those areas by improving manpower or by doing another campaign in that particular area could actually save the day. Sales monitoring reports would certainly go towards helping the companies in a big way.

Analysis and Calculating ROI:

A number of analyses are done in this model. First of all, after collecting the data from the market, call centre identifies prospects into different categories, like farmers below 5 acres, farmers up to 10 acres or more than 10 acres. Because of this analysis we could focus more on a particular segment than others. The conversion rate is identified for the focussed prospects and it is identified how many prospects are contacted. Once the sale is done we could actually find the conversion rate and also the cost per contact, cost per focussed contact and cost per sale. This data could be quite enlightening for the next campaigns.

Feedback and Planning for Next Season:

After the Project is over and sales are achieved, the next season planning and analysis can be done from the data which have been generated. As the data for the real users of the product is available, that can be used for up selling or cross selling. Even a loyalty program can be designed for the existing customers for the next season. A reference bonus for the customers who help to generate sales with references can also be generated.

The plan for next season can be to improve the conversion rate and maximise the ROI.

360 Degree Marketing and Sales Model an Example:

Product: Plant Growth Regulator (PGR)

State: Maharashtra

360 Degree Marketing and Sales Model align all the activities, agencies and vendors towards the achievement of the company's goal. This model helps to maximise the Return on Investment (ROI). The ROI is measured in real terms and is monitored on real time basis. The actions are taken accordingly in order to get desired results.

Elements of 360 Degree Marketing and Sales Model are:

- FA Costing
- Pop Materials
- Farmer Meeting
- Vehicle Campaigns
- Shop Branding
- Call Centre Operations

- Digital Campaigns
- Buffer Costings (can be used for Kissan Melas, TV advertisements)
  Target acres: 300,000

  Number of field assistants required: 30

  Farmers touched by 1 FA 25–30 villages: 3,000

  Average acres per village: 3,000

  Acres covered by 1 FA in 30 villages: 90,000

  Farmers touched by 30 FA 25–30 villages: 90,000

  Acres covered by 30 FA in 30 villages: 27, 00,000

  Total Focused Farmers (30% of Total): 30,000

  Acres owned by Focussed Farmers: 19, 00,000

(30% farmers own 70% of total land holding)

Conversion ratio of Touched Farmers: 11%

Conversion ratio of the Focused Farmers: 16%

This Model will be customised as per the product and the market.

OUTCOME

CHAPTER 15

Dos and Don'ts of Rural Campaigns

"Plan your work and work your plan"

– Napoleon Hill

The focus is on the importance of organising and taking action. Devising a rural marketing campaign can be challenging because of the many hurdles it brings along the way. The fact is that execution of any plan needs solid groundwork as well as scheduling of available resources in the rural areas and small towns. Conservatism states that it is necessary that plans should include detailed provisions for the unpredicted circumstances that may surface at the time of completion of the campaign. All that being said, prevention remains to be a better option than cure, however, the formation of such a strategy sounds very tiresome. It is nearly impossible to remember each and every detail while implementing a highly functional rural marketing campaign. The success rate of the execution of any strategy banks upon a list of dos and don'ts because it forms a loose boundary around the formations which is not rigid enough to distract creativity but clear enough to avoid mistakes.

The DOs

Branding on the Road from Village to City:

The economic activity is happening between the cities and villages where the customers from villages move towards the city to buy the products. So in order to influence the consumers, the branding is done on the roads which connects the village and the city. But here the important point to consider is the posters should be done in such a way that the posters should face the consumers when they are going towards the city not vice versa. As the posters will be acting as a reminder to the consumer just before he makes a buying decision. The other way of putting up posters will be a waste of money.

Selecting Correct Branding Period:

The period of branding in villages, shops and the pathways should be selected very appropriately. The shop branding should be done just 15 days before the actual sales start. The village branding should be done two months earlier to make it a talk of the town. Other activities like call centre activity, vehicle campaigns and boards in villages should be done two months earlier. The pathways should be branded 10 days before the actual sales start for the optimum utilisation of the resources.

Mixing Advertising Tools Optimally:

To pursue multiple ambitions, it is a prerequisite to know what comes first and what goes next and understand fully the reasons behind the same. For example, the client might be looking to target one particular market before others as per their overall strategic goals. Once the priority has been sorted out, the planning can start full throttle. The marketer should focus on all aspects of the campaign, such as content development, selection of mediums and searching out touch points. One area should not be given the majority of the focus but all of them should be given the due time and effort. The same should be done because every step is essential to create a successful rural marketing campaign. Any campaign cannot be designed without sufficient planning which starts with market research about the audience type, constructing marketing objectives which are realistic and ambitious at the same time. It mainly involves the drafting of a suitable marketing strategy fit for the brand and the product. Once the planning stage is over, the importance is transferred to preparing for the campaign to ensure its implementation without many surprises or hurdles. Given the benefits using technology can provide, it should not be ignored due to the campaign being rural. Rather a way should be found to use technology for increasing operational efficiency and effectiveness of the campaign. Integrate and align online and offline activation activities to reap best results. The 360 Degree Marketing and Sales model explained in Chapter14 could be one of the examples to use.

Identify the Decision Makers:

In every rural family there is a decision maker. Identifying the decision makers and connecting with them is always a challenge. A lot of farmer meetings are done but only 30% of them are farmers in those meetings and if we talk about influential farmers, they are not more than 5%. So in order to get real results of such meetings, we need to identify the real decision makers and contact them and showcase our product. Similar is the case with the influencer meetings, be it a mason's meet, an electrician's meet, a carpenter's meet, a beautician's meet or any other meet of such kind. In every such meeting, we need to take care that we are interacting with the right customer. Similarly while using the mass media or hoarding board positioning, we need to do the survey before installing in order to get the optimal impact.

Flexible Approach:

The major challenge in the rural market is that every market is still at the amateur stage. There are no set principles of successful campaigns. The changes in the campaigns are required as per the region and target segment. Sometimes there are instant requirements of the region and circumstances, which have to be fulfilled. The monsoon rains may intensify the seed sales in a particular region and advertising may be needed at the specific areas. Such situations regularly arise in rural marketing. An experienced and well connected agency is required for it.

Crisis Management:

While running a rural marketing campaign, performance indicators should be adopted. The calculation of ROI of the rural marketing campaign should be done by closely following numbers that show progress such as sales revenue, open rates, closure rates, value per lead, number of incremental contacts etc. This helps in understanding the results better and the crisis can be managed in a much better way if we have the measurements in hand. The local connects with the influencers play an important role in managing the crisis. The direct control over the local manpower is a must.

An advertising agency with rural roots is a must in such situations.

The DO'NTs

Do Not Move Out of Target Audience:

The target audience are the main focus of every campaign. But sometimes in the process of trying to cover more people, the campaigns go out of the target audience, thereby, wasting money and energy. Although the agency shows the ROI in terms of cost per connected consumer, to ensure that the connected person is a consumer or not is a very challenging question. Focussing on the right target segment and connecting the right consumers is very important. That is the reason why I always stress on sales in the ROI calculation.

Rural Areas Are Not Urban Areas:

Another common misconception among rural marketing agencies comes in the shape of believing that the lines between rural and urban markets have become completely blurred. While this may prove to be true after a decade, here and now, this approach can render your rural marketing campaign ineffective. Rural marketing starts with conversing to the customer whilst keeping their perception of the brand. The similarity in this connection cannot be established without the knowledge of the brand and the product itself. Therefore, the first and foremost rule of rural marketing is to pay attention to the client's requests and needs, rather than hearing them out, listen to them carefully.

Listen to the Customer Feedback:

Every single request, advice and feedback of the customer should be taken very seriously. Yes, it is true that the customer may not be aware of the product when compared to the company. However, they are the users of the product and understand its use, their insights can be very useful and these should be considered very carefully. The biggest mistake a rural marketing agency can make is failing to realise the importance of engaging content. The scope of content development goes beyond its digital presence and the understanding of the same can make a lot of difference in the performance of the campaign. The engaging content actually helps the customer to understand in a much better way. If the engagement even allows the feedback it would be an excellent way to connect with the customer, building a loyalty at the next level. If a customer gives any feedback, the company should revert back in any way. And if somebody gives a valuable feedback, the customer should be awarded and even used as an influencer. These activities will actually create a brand loyalty in a much better way.

Content and Vernaculars are Important:

The importance of vernaculars have been discussed in many parts of this book. The content in vernaculars is required for every campaign in the rural India. But here I want to discuss about the translation or the dubbing we do in local languages. The translation should not be done just literally but the essence of the message should also be taken care of. The homogeneity in the branding is very important for brand building, but keeping the essence of the message intact is equally important. Otherwise, the effectiveness of the message may reduce. Even the literal translation could be disastrous as well. The translation of the content should be taken care of very minutely and carefully.

Dilemma of Over or Under Budgeting:

Thou shall not commit the cardinal sin of over budgeting or under budgeting. While spending too much is considered wrong, not agreeing to pay enough can also affect the campaign negatively. The right way is to be cautious in your spending but be firm to not let it affect the quality of your work. Over or under budgeting in a particular advertising service can also be harmful. The optimal mix of the budget is advised.

Do Not Mix Campaign with Religion:

Sometimes advertisers try to connect too closely with the customers through close contact with religion, but this can be dangerous. Sometimes, even using the religious identity to connect with brand can also backfire. The image used to connect with culture may cause a lot of damage to the brand, so using such images and connecting it with the brand, one certainly needs to be very careful. For such experiments a local designer or a local consultant is a must.

CHAPTER 16

Challenges to Overcome in Rural India

The rural Indian market is growing at a rapid pace. They need many products and the choices of rural consumers are transforming drastically. So, rural marketing is becoming important in today's competitive market. Different services and products are being offered to rural folks. They may or may not be different from the ones in urban areas. But altogether different strategy is required to promote and market them. To face these challenges, marketers are using a combination of advertising and promotional techniques and also unique media communications for rural areas. With the rise in rural consumption, there has been a lot of discussion on marketing in villages. Rural India presents immense opportunity, but there are unique challenges that the area presents and need to be cautious. Spurious products, lower priced look alike and the challenge of reaching the last mile have always kept companies on their toes. Correct pricing and the scaling up in larger areas need to be really cautious about not losing money. The rural markets are credit markets and the payment collection have always been a challenge. I am sharing my experience which I have gained after multiple years of running campaigns.

Spurious and Me Too Brands:

The brands face a fierce competition from the spurious and me-too products in the market. These products are locally manufactured and are supplied to the retailers directly. They use the similar packages of the brands and look alike and use similar names, for example, 'Dabaar Aamlaa' and many others like this. These products are sold by retailers because of the lack of awareness at the rural level. Secondly, the lack of reach of the brands at the deep rural level also affects their sale at that level. Product awareness and reach is required by the brands to pick up sales in rural areas. Me-too brands work in small areas and they do appropriate branding there. With a strong workforce in small areas and low prices they pose a strong competition to the brands. I will cite an example here. L&T sells switches for the motors and pumps which are used in farms. In Punjab, they were faced with a fierce competition by one of the me-too brands. This brand was offering a lower price and offering exchange of the product if any problem occurred. Whereas although L&T was present in the market for more than 50 years, their connection with the customer was almost lost. The product, however, was working well wherever installed from the last twenty years in some cases. Due to the hyper activeness of the me-too brand and low activity of L&T, sales was hit. They approached us for a solution. We surveyed and analysed that L&T needed an awareness campaign for the brand. We started the awareness and focussed on the USPs of the product. We connected with the potential targets and the results started showing. The brands need to reinvent themselves regularly in order to remain strong. This is quite a challenge for companies.

Logistics and Distribution:

Lack of proper infrastructure is a top challenge in Indian villages. Secondly, lack of efficient distribution system hampers the reach of services/products into rural Indian villages. One of the models in recent times has been the usage of the Indian postal service by mobile companies to penetrate scratch cards to the rural areas. The mighty Indian Postal Service with more than 1,50,000 post offices is the largest distribution network across the globe and has more than 120000 centres in India's villages. Another challenge is the small usage by the rural villages does not make a full truckload and hence becomes expensive logistically to distribute the material at every corner. With the advent of Tata Ace, also called 'Chota Hathi,' some problems have been resolved. The companies need to build the warehouses in the 200 km area so that the material should reach in a few hours. The use of appropriate vehicle can also reduce the cost of logistics. Quicker supply can also help in improving the sales. Still logistics and distribution is quite a challenge for many companies. I believe that logistics intertwined with technology can solve it in a much better way.

Payment Collection and Credit Market:

Times are changing very fast, Indian villages are connecting with banks. Reduction in usage of cash has started but still we have to go a long way. The real challenge in the rural markets is that largely the markets are agriculture dependent and credit is required at every step. The rural markets need credit from companies as well and sometimes the payment collection becomes really difficult, especially when there is a stress in the market like monsoon delays or rains at wrong times. It creates a lot of pressure on the trading community and they are not able to pay at the right time. Selection of the distributors is also a quite a challenge in these areas. The proven manufacturer, distributor and retailer network has been the only success so far, although setting up such a structure is quite difficult.

Pricing:

The price is the value a customer pays for what he gets as a package of utility, honour and satisfaction. While pricing a product all these three values should be considered. Normally a price is calculated with the costs plus the profit. But this is not the real way to do it. The price depends on multiple factors and the affordability comes last. The first one is the need of that product. The larger the need, more the value it creates. Secondly, how critical the product is for the customer. A particular pesticide may be required at a critical stage of the crop where the farmer cannot take a risk, the value of the product automatically rises and so the price. Here the price is not calculated with the profits generated rather what benefit it gives to the farmer. Thirdly, the point of affordability comes in. But there are many other factors behind the process of pricing. The study of the competition market and placing your brand in that bandwidth is again a very challenging task. Understanding your brand value and positioning it in resonance with brand value is the key to pricing. The lower pricing could hit the margins and devalue the product. Whereas over pricing could be the reason for loss of sale. So pricing is one of the critical steps in the rural marketing jargon.

Scaling Up in Other Markets:

India is a country of different cultures, the trend becomes even more scattered in the case of remote villages. Setting up business operations on a PAN-India level encounters different kinds of issues in various states ranging from social to political factors. Any business model where scalability means scaling on real grounds, operations is bound to run into unknown issues as we switch from one state to the other. Add to it the differences in consumer priorities and behaviour across locations than in the relatively less scattered urban Indian population. The heterogeneity and diversity in the country creates many challenges for companies to move forward and expand. Few factors need to be considered before starting the expansion. Analysis of the strength of the market for a particular product is required, whether a similar product can be delivered or if some cosmetic or other changes are required. LG electronics gives different designs for different regions of India after studying requirement and liking of specific regions. This strategy has worked well for LG. Another factor could be the affordability of that product in that particular region. The development levels, job opportunities and the life style of the people of that area are also important factors. The awareness levels and adaptation to new technologies is also a major factor for launching a new product in a particular region. The demography, seasonal study and the crop pattern is also an important factor to be considered. A particular agricultural machinery is required in one region and another in the other region. Developing artificial scale through partnerships has resulted in growing overheads in the rural Indian market. Finding the right person with reach in villages is not so easy to start with. Moreover, there are very few companies who are strong on these people across multiple areas. Hence, a whole India roll out requires multiple strong partnerships resulting in growing partner management overhead costs. So the scalability is not just a cut paste job in rural India but needs a lot of research and analysis before going for it.

Picking Up Pace:

The growth in sales is the dream of every organisation. Improvement in sales can be done in three ways, by cross selling the existing customers, adding new customers and expanding in new areas. The expansion challenges have been discussed in the earlier paragraph.

The cross selling and adding new customer in the same geography is the best way to improve sales without adding much to the overheads. Cross selling is selling another product to the existing customer. This can be done by leveraging the brand value of the existing product for the customer. For that we could generate the database of the existing customers by using code based packing and luring the customer to send the code on a particular number. We can lure the customer through a lucky draw or assured prize for every code sent. We will be able to collect the users' numbers and can push our other products for sale to the existing customers. We could do this with digital technology and even build an ecosystem for customer entertainment, satisfaction and finally delight. Here, the chances of sales are very high. Adding new customers is always a challenging preposition. But focusing on the right set of consumers through target focusing methodology we could influence them through multiple campaigns. The best being 360 Degree Sales and Marketing Model as explained earlier in this book. The acquisition of new customers is always a bit expensive but long term engagement could give fantastic results in the form of brand value and brand loyalty. The selection of the geographical areas in the form of clusters will benefit the most as the communication will be percolated around the cluster automatically making it a branding success leading to sales explosion.

Social and Cultural Challenges:

The socio cultural fabric of India is very diverse and it poses a lot of challenges for the companies and the marketers. The patriarchal society makes half of the population powerless and stops them from using their full potential for growth. Women now have started rising educationally and financially which have changed the scenario. But reaching women for the products related to them is still a challenge. Taking an example of kiosk model, the kiosk model has successfully worked in some parts and not worked in other parts of rural India due to socio cultural fabric. One of the prime reasons for the fall down of the kiosk model was the lack of usage by women, reason being their discomfort in going to kiosks run by opposite gender. Similarly the social structure of caste system in our society have destroyed the self-confidence of almost 60% of population which comprise of the lower class, although with reservation and other government policies they have started rising. With the advent of lower caste leaders in politics, the self-confidence of these classes have started rising. But still educational backwardness rules the roost. Reaching the lower classes is still a challenge. Around 70% of the population is under poverty line and expecting demand generation from such families will be a futile exercise. In order to build this country into a developed nation we need to work on our poor. I don't, at any point, want to play down the potential that is present. Most of the points just go back to the basic assumption that rural India is a volume market and need scale that is organically the largest challenge. The ones who will succeed in solving these problems will definitely change the world around us. The target behind all these efforts is to create awareness and changing spending habits among farmers and others about bank services and benefits. These challenges create a lot of trouble for the marketers in rural India.

CHAPTER 17

Campaign Effectiveness Techniques

Marketers of rural India believe strongly about the advertising media. They think about advertising to create awareness about the product. Various strategies are used to advertise and various methodologies are applied in rural advertising. While doing all this, few important factors should be taken into account and those factors are critically important to make the campaigns highly effective. The branding and the placement needs a perfect resonance in order to optimise the results. The brand definitely needs a robust retailer support in order to reach the masses. The advertising and branding activities are required not only for brand visibility but should be focussed on liquidation as well. The customer connection is the foremost activity in any campaign but for any brand to survive the customer retention is always a challenge. We can use the customer reference for a better reach. With more and more usage of internet by the customers, the use of Artificial Intelligence and interactive marketing could be the key in the coming days. The data collection and using it for the demand generation could be of great importance for success in Rural Marketing.

Branding and Placement Resonance:

Another important activity after appointment of distributors or retailers is placement. Placement means transporting the product from the company's warehouse to the retailer's shelf where a customer can see or get the product when he or she demands it. Any campaign without proper placement leads to a wastage of money and effort leading to low ROI. Even if the customer enquires about the product after being influenced by the advertisement campaign and the product is not placed, that will lead to dissatisfaction and bad reputation for the company in the eyes of the customer as well as the retailer.

All the activities should be done after the placement is proper and the product is visible. Some advertisers or marketing strategists do use a teaser campaign to raise the curiosity levels in the consumer's mind. In this case the data of the interested customers can be collected and they can be contacted after the product is available. It may help to make the brand to become the talk of the town but the company will surely lose sales as these days a lot of options are available and the customer does not like to wait.

Retailer Support:

The distributor retailer network development is the most crucial phase for any company and this phase is a continuous development. The company has to build proper retailer network for the distribution of the product so that the product is readily available at the doorstep of the rural populace. Success of any advertising campaign directly depends on the strength of the retailer network of the company. So selection of the distributors and the retailers is most crucial for any campaign's success. The selection process should be based on multiple criteria. The experience of the distributor in the business, the brands he has already handled, his financial health and his reputation in the market, the retailer network he owns, etc. can be useful criteria for appointment. Even the area of campaign should be selected on the basis of the distributor's team in that area. The first and the heaviest campaign should be done in the areas where the company has the best retailer and distributor presence. Such activities will give highest ROI and the expense will be much lower. This strategy will help the brand to achieve a place in the customer's mind. Many companies focus only on the distributors, but the real liquidation happens at the retailer level. So the details about the retailers should be captured and the sales happening at his counter should be monitored closely. The detailed strategy for the selection of area is already given in the chapter 14, 360 Degree Marketing and Sales Model.

Liquidity Oriented Branding Activities:

Advertising is a balance between clear communication and creativity. Sometimes the advertisers in the pursuit of creativity lose the real communication behind the advertisement. In my view, the communication should be very clear in the case of rural advertisements. As the customers are very simple and straightforward, therefore, they like straight forward communication. Creativity can be inculcated only after considering the culture and the target audience.

Real branding activity is the sale of the product, so the most important job in any advertising campaign is that the campaign should be liquidity oriented which means that the element of sales or the capturing of leads should always be there. The rural campaigns should be designed in such a way that it leads to direct liquidation of the product. There are multiple examples for such activities like lucky draw coupons at exhibitions for the prospects converting to customers, lead generation during the vehicle campaign, and many others.

Customer Connection and Retention:

The acquisition of the customer has always been very important but the retention of the customer is much more critical for the growth of the company. The focus on the retention is increasing day by day. In urban markets, loyalty points are given by many retail stores and credit card companies to retain the customers. But in rural markets, because of its vastness and colossal size, it is difficult to keep an eye on the customer retention numbers. Still some campaigns for the customer retention are done by many companies. Some seed companies focus on the customer farmers in the fields to show their seed's performance through field days. In the field days they honour the farmers who follow best practices, leading to retention.

A strategy can be used for the retention of the customers for rural markets. A unique code is printed on every pack and a communication is printed that a lucky draw or a prize is awaiting for him if he sends the code to a specific number. That specific number is used to collect the mobile numbers of customers using technology. Even we can calculate how many packs a particular customer has bought. We can analyse the data and categorise the customers. This data can be used for the next campaigns and cross selling. A loyalty program can be used as well. We can pitch for the complete kit of products to the customers leading to cross-selling and up-selling.

Customer Reference:

Reference is the best advertising and prospecting. In the advertising campaigns, the reference campaign should always be an important part. The reference will lead to much higher lead generation. The incentives on reference generation can even improve the brand loyalty. The reference can be generated through a technological strategy where every customer is sent a message asking reference numbers from him for which he will get the loyalty points. In order to do so, first you have to find out the numbers of the real customers who have already bought your material. I have given that strategy in the previous paragraph. Once the customer has the trust that the loyalty program actually works, then he will be excited to give reference numbers. Contacting the references using the customer's name can do wonders. Improving the customer base using these strategies can be very helpful.

Role of Artificial Intelligence (AI):

In computer science, artificial intelligence, sometimes called machine intelligence, is intelligence demonstrated by machines, in contrast to the natural intelligence displayed by humans and animals. This is the general definition of artificial intelligence. The use of machine learning to convert the data into knowledge is the Artificial Intelligence (AI). AI developers are working on areas including manufacturing, logistics, supply chains, urban transportation, business processes, healthcare, asset management, and more. The use of AI in rural marketing and other operations will be visible in the next few years.

In the marketing perspective, interaction through bots have already started but still many marketing companies have to start using such technologies. The use of bots where the bots will interact with the customers by identifying their questions and answering them in person will be a reality very soon. As the AI takes over the technology or digital avatars will start answering the most tedious questions with such ease when fed with knowledge. The day is not far away when the digital avatars will start interacting like experts in the field. As an agency, we are working on it and will be able to give a solution by the end of this year.

Digitalisation of the Outdoor Campaigns:

The outdoor campaigns have always been the back bone of rural marketing. But the campaigns are now becoming more and more monotonous. The improvement in the effectiveness of such campaigns is seriously required. The outdoor campaigns like vehicle campaign, hoardings, shop branding, mandi campaigns, wall paintings etc. are many ways to reach or influence the rural customer. But now the time has come when we need to digitalise them and connect them with technology. The vehicle campaigns can be connected with the web servers through which vehicle tracking, data capturing and virtual interaction can be done from remote places. We can also use an AI avatar to interact with the customers and answer their queries through knowledge management. Similar digitalisations can also be done for the interactive boards or kiosks in the retailer shops or in the mandis.

Data Collection and Analysis:

Prospect data collection is done in almost every activity and most of the companies have collected good amount of data. The method used for data collection is normally manual where the field staff collects the mobile numbers of the farmers, village wise. In such collection methods, many errors happen and around 80% of the data is incorrect due to human errors. This data collection can be changed from manual mode to digital mode. We can use the missed call on a particular number which is noted on the server where all the calls are logged. The logged calls can then be called back or a WhatsApp message sent or SMS for data capturing.

We can capture the data via WhatsApp where the person will get a WhatsApp message instantly and the bot will start interacting and will start collecting the data which will be submitted by the farmer himself.

Such activities will improve the efficiency and reduce the errors. The data collected can be analysed instantaneously and the customers can be categorised. This categorisation will decide to what extent each customer can be pushed for conversion. Such campaigns are possible only through digital technologies.

We can use digital technologies in many ways where the virtual interaction and customer loyalty programs can be propagated through technology. There by using multiple techniques for campaign effectiveness whereby we can improve our efficiency multi fold. I will be regularly talking about new ideas on my blogs which you can find on www.sarabsays.com.

CHAPTER 18

Role of AI in Rural Marketing

AI represents Artificial Intelligence. AI is used for machine learning. This technology can be used in any form. AI is the program which helps the machine to respond like a human in specific circumstances. I have listed some types of AI. Logical AI is when a program knows how to act in a specific situation and its goals are all represented by sentences of mathematical logical language. The program decides what to do by inferring that certain actions are appropriate for achieving its goals. The search AI programs examine large number of possibilities, e.g. moves in a game. Discoveries are continuously made about how to do this more efficiently in various domains. Pattern recognition is done using AI where it is programmed to compare what it sees in a pattern. For example, a vision program may try to match a pattern of eyes and a nose in a scene in order to find a face. More complex patterns, e.g. in a language text, in a complex position, etc. The AI is used for representation of facts in some way. Usually languages of mathematical logic are used. The inference from some facts can be done. In the case of common sense and reasoning, AI is farthest from human-level, in spite of the fact that it has been an active research area since the 1950s. While there has been considerable progress, e.g. in developing systems of non-monotonic reasoning and theories of action, yet more new ideas are needed. AI actually now moves to a new level of learning from experience. Programs can only learn what facts or behaviours their formalisms can represent and these are used in many social media sites and by telecom companies to study behaviours of the consumers and specific advertisements and information is pushed to them. We will discuss this in this chapter. There are other forms of AI as well like planning programs, epistemology, ontology, heuristics, and genetic programming. The role of AI has started in marketing and rural market will get a great push through integrating AI with digital and other conventional methods.

Reaching Masses through Technology:

The rural marketers have been using outdoor and the mass media to reach out to the customer. Rural call centres, SMS campaigns and the voice blast have been used for interacting with the masses. These media have many challenges as far as reach is concerned. The digital media like social media and other such platforms like Facebook page, Instagram, WhatsApp, company's digital platforms offer engagement and interaction with each and every user available there. This strength of the technology to interact and engage with the consumer is amazing. The webinars, virtual meetings and the two way communications with millions of customers is possible only through technology. With the rise in the use of smart phones in rural India, connecting with rural India has become much easier and comparatively at a lower cost. We could improve the reach and effectiveness by integrating all the digital platforms, outdoor campaigns and the mass media campaigns. This would help us to improve the connectivity, engagement and two way interaction with the customer leading to better lead generation and better conversion rate. This is explained in 360 degree Digital Lead Generation Model in Chapter 12.

Connecting Social Media Using APIs:

Social media is used a lot by rural India and connecting rural through social media will be an advantage. Just putting a page on Facebook or just sending WhatsApp messages won't work now. With the rise in technology and opening up of APIs of WhatsApp and Facebook, it would actually help the brands to connect and interact with the customers. This connection and interaction can be machine based using bots and if the customer shows curiosity, then the human can come and convert the sale.

Now with the rise in AI tools for the interaction with the customers, the tools will be self-learning with the experience and these tools can answer much more accurately with time. Even the satellite services can be fetched, analysed, processed and presented to the customer with the help of AI. We could provide services like the land analysis in the form of fertiliser utilisation, water requirement and weather in local areas, etc. These solutions with the help of AI could connect much more customers with the brand and would lead to better sales, credibility and longer engagement and trust.

Reducing Response Time Using Bots:

If a customer is connecting with you in the form of liking your information, or writing a comment to interact or sharing the information to his timeline or page or a WhatsApp peer group, he should be responded to immediately and his details should be captured immediately. The details can be captured and the interaction would start in his FB Messenger or on his WhatsApp with the help of the technology called bots. These bots are the programs which are pre fed with the information to be sent immediately when a customer interacts with the system in any form. The bots can provide various options to the customer and even he could interact in his own language for better understanding. The normal bots can act like answering the FAQs or IVRs but the AI enabled bots could start learning with the experience and could be quite an expert in the field with time. We could connect with more number of customers using bots and could generate much more leads than the humans on the job. This could also reduce the sales agent's work and he could accomplish much more with the help of this technology. Secondly, once a customer is connected with any of the platforms through bots, he could get and fetch information any time and with different ways we could engage him in a much better way and for a longer period of time.

Digital Platforms for Customer Engagement:

360 Degree digital marketing platform is used to integrate all the digital media connected with the company. It helps the different media to talk to each other and improves the interaction capability of every media. This platform is installed on the cloud server or in-house server, but cloud server will be much cheaper and easier to handle. This platform

builds an ecosystem for the customers and other stakeholders where the company could send the information capsules frequently. Here, the customers can interact freely with the company by liking the information, replying on it with a feedback or suggestion or could ask a question for its requirement. The customers will be engaged with the help of bots. The platform engages with the customers using easy forms, polls, spin wheel games and many other such activities. Live webinar sessions can happen on the platform and the link of these live sessions can be sent across the media for better reach. Rural TV – Installation and Customisation of Video Streaming Service and the webinars are recorded and saved here for the anytime use for the rural customers. These videos are streamed and can be seen at any point of time. The best part is that the digital platforms offer all the services in all the languages of the world so that the company could build the customers' ecosystem in their language for better connectivity. The leads from all the digital media are captured here and are transferred to the rural call centres for further filtering.

Integrating Call Centres with Digital Leads:

Dedicated rural call centre work for one business only. Dedicated agents are trained specifically to provide service for your business, incorporating your branding and image into the service they provide. With a dedicated rural agent, your company essentially has its own customer service representatives. While many large businesses use dedicated call centre agents to handle high volumes of calls, more small businesses are beginning to use this option to their advantage. The customers are handled through calling and different channels such as social media and WhatsApp or SMS campaigns. The requests and messages are directly replied and treated with. The integration of call centre with the digital platform will create a 360 degree approach of capturing leads via all digital, outdoor and call centre channels. All the leads captured and engaged by the digital platforms are transferred to the call centres for further filtration and these filtered leads will either be converted through call centres only or will be transferred to the field staff. The call centre handles the language-wise leads and the human touch at the closing of the lead will create a lot of satisfaction at the customer level. Even the retailer could be involved in the sale. Digital platforms are a viable marketing tool and can be used to increase customer loyalty because it allows businesses to communicate directly with their customers via purchases, ads, promotions and notifications sent to customers via the digital platform. These four benefits of the digital platform demonstrates the importance of developing a 360 degree digital platform for your company. The most useful function is to build and cultivate customer loyalty. Platforms tend to be more accessible and interactive than a traditional website. Enhance your accessibility and reach. Make your brand more human and adding an emotional touch helps to build a database of new prospects or clients. Platforms allow for capturing more data than websites. Companies want the maximum data they can get about potential customer. This allows them to tailor the experience they provide to the customer so that he spends more time with the platform and are more likely to use some of the more obscure features.

Data Analytics:

We can't improve what we can't measure. The measurement and then the processing followed by analysis is the most important part of any marketing activity. Today with large number of customers and stiff competition, data analysis with a human workforce could be a challenge. An essential component of ensuring data integrity is the accurate and appropriate analysis of research findings. Data Analysis using AI is the process of systematically applying statistical and/or logical techniques to describe and illustrate, condense and recap and evaluate data. The process of data analysis uses analytical and logical reasoning to gain information from the data. Data analysis has two prominent methods: qualitative research and quantitative research. Each method has their own techniques. Interviews and observations are forms of qualitative research, while experiments and surveys are quantitative research. The main purpose of data analysis is to find meaning in data so that the derived knowledge can be used to make informed decisions. Data collection and analysis tools are defined as a series of charts, maps and diagrams designed to collect, interpret and present data for a wide range of applications and industries.

The data analysis in the case of marketing is first capturing data automatically as mentioned earlier. The captured data is filtered and then converted into leads. These conversions help us to calculate ROI. The marketer's challenge would always be to improve that ROI. So to improve that, data analysis needs to be done. Data analysis clearly illustrates about which campaigns have given better ROIs than the other campaigns. The optimum usage of budgets and creating maximum ROI is the basic aim for data analysis. With the help of AI tools, the analysis could be much more effective and accurate.

CHAPTER 19

Choosing the Right Agency and Maximising ROI

A careful selection of the advertising and marketing agency is the key to success in the rural market. The rural agency with a rural team, who has an experience in rural parts would be the best people to do the work. Rural India being very diverse, needs a national presence in all parts of the country to execute the plan required. Even in the case of digital strategy, different language wise pages are required to be maintained and that can be done locally. The agency needs to be experienced enough so that the strategy should integrate with the local conditions. The practical implementation of the strategy at the local level is a must. The agency with robust processes in place would be able to do much better in implementation than the agency without any processes. The agency with local presence and with its own operations will be much better in implementation than just strategists dependent on the local vendors of low efficiency. The selection of the agency can be done on the basis of the following factors.

Rural Team Is a Must:

The most important part to be observed about the rural agency is that whether its team is rural or not. The team members with rural base and experience would certainly make the difference. This is not just about having a degree in rural MBA or an agricultural degree, but to understand the culture, the language, the emotions and the fads in rural India. These strengths in the team is a must. The team players should have worked in those areas for minimum 5 years and have travelled length and breadth of the area understanding the crop patterns, youth aspirations and the living standards of the people of that region. The growth in the technology adaptation, the thought process and the mind-set of the rural people of the region are some of the most important aspects the team members should study and understand. These points are very important. The study of any brand and its competitors in that region which require introspection and feedback from the retailers and the end users. While studying the position of the brand in a particular region a strong team player is required.

National Presence with Regional Connect:

In order to build a brand across the country, the agency should understand every part of the country. This is possible only if the agency is working in all the regions and has a presence there. The agency should have their own office and presence and the basic works should be done by the agency itself. Many agencies are simply dependent on outsourcing to the inefficient vendors in local areas and try to control through a head office or office in a Tier II or Tier I city. This strategy do not work well. The reach of such agencies is till the Tier III towns only and villages are far away from them. The regional connect is a must for the agency to work in rural areas.

All Services in One Bouquet:

There are multiple things which a company does to build a brand. Some of them are mass media campaigns, outdoor campaigns, social media campaigns, digital efforts like Social Media Integration and SEO, call centres in multiple languages, etc. But are all these aligned properly to generate leads and convert them into sales? This is the real question. The alignment will help in designing the campaigns in such a way that every campaign is complimenting each other. In this strategy, the different channels, be it outdoor, mass media, different digital channels, call centre, etc. talk to each other and generate leads. The agency having all these services in their bouquet would be able to implement this in a much better way than the agency with few services with them. The presence in all regions is an all important aspect.

Implementation at Local Level:

Planning and strategy might be great. However, success completely depends on implementation. And the implementation is always at the local level in the case of rural advertising and marketing. The implementing agency needs to be practical and present at the local level. The agency should understand and know whether the planned things would be implemented or not, if yes then how. So if the planning and implementing teams are aligned then the results will certainly be wonderful and best. And if the agency is same the chances are much better. So I suggest the companies to connect with a single agency for complete marketing campaign across the country for better results.

Vernacular Teams at Local Level:

Translation in the local language has always been a challenge for every company. The translations can't be done on a literal basis as sometimes the essence of the message gets diluted, so does the effectiveness in the campaign. So the translation needs to be done at the local level where people understand the culture and the dialect of that region. If I take an example Hindi is one language but every region like west UP, east UP, Chhattisgarh, Bihar, etc. have different dialects. So should the translation be. The special focus on the translation and its message is very important. In the case of vernaculars, it is not the perfect language that works rather the dialect used by the people. The dialect changes with some distance so the variation has to be considered. The communication should be made in every dialect where the brand is to be positioned. In the case of visuals like still pictures or videos, we should be very careful. While making a TV advertisement or a video, the video should not be dubbed. Rather reshooting should be done with local cultural elements in place with the universal communication. These can only be done if the agency understands all the regions where it operates and has a local presence. The local team of the agency can coordinate with the local team of the brand leading for better effectiveness while implementation. The agency with national coverage and local presence could do wonders. The brand manager should select such an agency.

Local Coordination:

The agency needs to implement the campaigns on the local level. All outdoor campaigns are to be coordinated on the local level basis and need a lot of coordination with the company's team for better ROI. The communication is required to be in the local language so the translation also needs to be done at local levels to keep the essence of the communication intact. Even in the case of videos, the local actors with local communication should be used so that the advertisement connects perfectly with the people for better impact and ROI. Although a digital campaign can be run from central location but still it needs an input from local marketing and agency teams for the better implementation. Secondly in the case of digital marketing, the visuals are in local languages. Local language pages should be created on Facebook, Instagram etc. In order to manage them the local team would be a much better preposition than a person sitting in the national office. The regional team reports to the national team and a coordination is a must. The agency with such facilities at local level should be preferred.

Strong Processes:

An agency with strong processes at every stage would certainly give better results. Advertising agency working in larger areas must have ERP. Such agencies with defined processes measure every action and its results. The measurement is the most important aspect for maximising ROI. The process oriented agencies connect better with the processes of the client companies. The deliverables, roles and responsibilities are fixed in order to strengthen the process. The selection of agency on this basis can also be a good way. Some agencies sitting in metro cities tie up with unorganised cheap local vendors for the execution. These agencies no doubt use best of the processes but the local vendors don't have any idea about them. As the implementation completely depend on them affects its effectiveness. Some care should also be taken while selecting the agency. Such urban agencies should be avoided. Selecting an agency with rural roots and own implementing teams would be ideal.

Building Practical Strategy:

Practical strategy which will help in building brand and capturing leads in every activity would certainly help the companies in improving their sales. The capturing process could be automatic and handled through digital and other channels. The practicality and simplicity of the plan is a must for its implementation. The practical plans can be made by the agencies who have experience of implementing them at multiple levels. The agencies with good experience should be connected for better results in rural India.

I have been running the advertising and marketing agency since 2002 with the name of Fateh Rural Pvt Ltd. We, as a team, have implemented multiple projects and have built many brands from scratch. Our clients include many MNCs and national companies. We have multiple regional offices and we are completely a process-oriented company with a complete ERP in place. We offer bouquet of services including designing, outdoor, mass media, digital, rural call centres and many more. We offer complete 360 degree lead generation sales and marketing model which aligns all the activities of branding and captures the leads and engages the consumers for brand building for longer durations.

Fateh Rural (www.fatehrural.com) is an agency for marketing in the rural world.

My Journey

The road I have travelled as an entrepreneur…

I started my career as an entrepreneur, learnt skills of handling and making business successful in the course of time from the college called "Market."

The entrepreneurial spirit was always there in me. I never had a job anywhere. I started my venture just after my graduation at my hometown, Bathinda, Punjab. I founded *Fateh Rural* as a private limited company in 2003 and have run it profitably for all these years. Fateh grew from a single office in a small town in Punjab to a corporate spanning across the country, having operations in 35+ towns and more than 10 regional offices with the head office at Fort, Mumbai, India. We, as a company, have been able to add almost all major services in our bouquet that is required for marketing and sales in Rural India. Our niche was always rural and we have grown in this arena. We have built many brands during our journey and have run thousands of campaigns during all these years.

The list of customers make us proud. Almost all major multinationals in agrochemical and other sectors, to name a few, Bayer, Syngenta, L&T, Godrej and many more belong in our client portfolio. We have 100+ corporate customers now. Innovating, trying to understand market changes and experimenting have helped us to grow. We believe in learning from the professionals and co-learning is the DNA of the company. We have been able to build an amazing team, many of our team members are with us for the last 15 years.

The experience I have gained is from travelling and meeting people. I have been moving around India by road. I have travelled more than 5 lakh kilometres. I have seen the length and breadth of the country and have interacted with thousands of farmers, rural people, distributors, retailers, different categories of people in order to understand the local level of economic development, type of crops, technology they are exposed to and which particular product they are using and what is the average income or average land owned by farmers in that area. Experiencing and understanding *Bharat,* I have worked closely with many MNC and National Brands for their development.

My personal mission is to integrate technology with conventional means of advertising.

We, as a company, have worked at the core rural levels, moving from village to village and catering to farmers, distributors and dealers in Tier II, III and IV towns of India.

In 2015, I founded *Green Orange HR Pvt Ltd* at Mumbai, India into HR services. Green Orange is a sister concern of Fateh Rural. We help companies in Payroll, Compliances, Placement, Training and Monitoring services in Rural India.

Future Aspirations:

- Expansion in Asia, Africa, South America, Europe, Australia and North America.

  Opening World Head Quarters at New York, USA.

- Exploring funding options for the expansion of Fateh Rural.

– Sarabjit Singh Puri

About Fateh Rural

Fateh is *winning rural markets* since 2002. Since the last 17 years, we have been working for Rural Market Branding for more than 100 multi-national and national companies including many Fortune 100 companies. We believe in reaching every rural corner of the world and reaching people at their doorsteps, using our rural infrastructural hubs at regional levels. We develop strategies and implement them at the rural level, delivering the products and brands at the doorstep of potential customers.

Fateh's team is headquartered at Mumbai and from 12 regional offices and 22 operating cities, expanding at a fast pace. Fateh believes in delighting customers in rural marketing by rendering services of the highest possible quality and quantity.

If you want to build the brand in Rural India, you need Fateh.

Our Major Services:

1. *360 Degree Digital Lead Generation Model*

2. *360 Degree Sales and Marketing Model*

3. Digital Marketing

4. Rural Call Centre Services (16 languages in India from multiple locations)

5. Outdoor Services (Vehicle Campaigns, Boards, Shop Branding, Hoardings)

6. Mass Media and Media Buying (National and Regional TV channels and Radio & FM)

7. Printing (Paper, Flex, etc.)

8. Gift Items

9. Rural Events

Contact: www.FatehRural.com

About Green Orange HR

Green Orange HR Pvt Ltd was registered in 2015 to support industry for the manpower supply, training and monitoring for Rural India. Green Orange has offices across India.

1. We provide following services for Rural HR:
2. We do Payroll Processing
3. We provide Manpower in Rural India
4. Trainings of Various Types
5. Team Monitoring
6. Project-wise Manpower Solutions

Some advantages are mentioned below:

- We provide monthly compliance reports to the clients.
- We also provide monthly payslips to each and every employee.
- Statutory Compliances like PF, ESIC, PT, LWF etc.
- We have State-wise Registrations for ESIC, PT, LWF

We use updated technology, we provide support via a portal which is directly connected on WhatsApp as well.

Contact: www.GreenOrangeHR.com

www.ingramcontent.com/pod-product-compliance
Lightning Source LLC
Chambersburg PA
CBHW021418210526
45463CB00001B/435